Soccer Restart Plays

2nd Edition

J. Malcolm Simon
John A. Reeves
Editors

Human Kinetics

Library of Congress Cataloging-in-Publication Data

Soccer restart plays / J. Malcolm Simon, John A. Reeves, editors. --
2nd ed.
p. cm.
ISBN 0-7360-0133-6
1. Soccer--Coaching. I. Simon, J. Malcolm. II. Reeves, John A.
(John Albert), 1939- .
GV943.8.S67 1999
796.334'07'7--dc21 99-12419
CIP

ISBN: 0-7360-0133-6

Acquisitions Editor: Jeff Riley; **Managing Editor:** Melinda Graham; **Assistant Editor:** Laurie Stokoe; **Copyeditor:** Marc Jennings; **Proofreader:** Sarah Wiseman; **Graphic Designer:** Nancy Rasmus; **Graphic Artist:** Francine Hamerski; **Photo Editor:** Clark Brooks; **Cover Designer:** Jack Davis; **Photographer (cover):** ©Allsport; **Illustrator:** Sharon Smith; **Printer:** Versa Press

Human Kinetics books are available at special discounts for bulk purchase. Special editions or book excerpts can also be created to specification. For details, contact the Special Sales Manager at Human Kinetics.

Printed in the United States of America 10 9 8 7 6 5 4 3 2 1

Human Kinetics
Web site: http://www.humankinetics.com/

United States: Human Kinetics, P.O. Box 5076, Champaign, IL 61825-5076
1-800-747-4457
e-mail: humank@hkusa.com

Canada: Human Kinetics, 475 Devonshire Road Unit 100, Windsor, ON N8Y 2L5
1-800-465-7301 (in Canada only)
e-mail: humank@hkcanada.com

Europe: Human Kinetics, P.O. Box IW14, Leeds LS16 6TR, United Kingdom
+44 (0) 113-278 1708
e-mail: humank@hkeurope.com

Australia: Human Kinetics, 57A Price Avenue, Lower Mitcham, South Australia 5062
(08) 82771555
e-mail: humank@hkaustralia.com

New Zealand: Human Kinetics, P.O. Box 105-231, Auckland Central
09-523-3462
e-mail: humank@hknewz.com

To all the soccer players it has been our privilege to coach

Contents

Foreword

How important are soccer's restart plays? France won the 1998 World Cup by beating four-time champion Brazil, 3-0, on the strength of two goals via corner kicks. In a second-round victory, Brazil scored on three free kicks—including a penalty kick.

So how important is *Soccer Restart Plays* to your soccer team?

The 128 restart plays that are expertly diagrammed and described in this book will help win games for your team. The plays are provided by 60 of the game's finest coaches, whose insight will help you develop your strategic plan on both sides of scrimmage.

In this edition, Mal Simon and John Reeves added 12 plays, including several essential free kicks, corner kicks, throw-ins, and kickoffs that will undoubtedly bolster your team's game plan. Each play is exquisitely diagrammed and aptly detailed.

The plays also include tips for determining the best use of an offensive play, using defense strategies that will help you anticipate and adjust to common defensive formations, and determining which weather conditions are the best for certain plays and how to compensate for windy or rainy conditions. Additionally, you'll learn how to assess your ability to execute plays based on your players' strengths and weaknesses.

You don't have to coach at the World Cup level to know that many soccer matches are won by the team that better executes its set plays. By implementing the plays in this book, you'll give your team a decided advantage.

We've won four national championships and made 12 Final Four appearances at Indiana, thanks in part to several of the restart plays that are outlined in this book—including one particular favorite, Back Door the Wall, on page 17. Give your team a similar advantage by putting *Soccer Restart Plays* to work for you.

– Jerry Yeagley
Indiana University

Preface

Goal! Nothing is more satisfying to a team's players and coaches, nor as exciting to its supporters, than a goal scored from a well-planned and well-executed restart play. The importance of restart plays in scoring goals cannot be overemphasized. More than a third of all goals—and often the deciding goals—are scored from restarts. A restart play, especially from scoring vicinity, is always better than an aimless kick. Such opportunities are too valuable to waste.

As in past World Cups, World Cup '98 vividly portrayed the importance of restart plays. These accounted for many goals scored; more than once, the deciding goal. France won its first World Cup, defeating four-time World Cup champion Brazil 3-0, with the first two goals coming from corner kicks. Brazil scored on three free kicks—including one penalty kick—in the first half of a 4-1 second-round victory over Chile. The United States fell victim to game-winning restart-play goals in losses to Germany and Yugoslavia. Descriptions of these and other goals scored from restart plays during World Cup '98 are in chapters 1 and 3.

Although soccer, unlike American football, is not a set-play type of game, every contest provides frequent opportunities to use restart plays. When the action stops and a restart is needed to get the ball moving again, you should carefully plan and execute the play. *Soccer Restart Plays* will teach you how.

This book includes 80 plays and 48 variations for free kicks, corner kicks, throw-ins, and kickoffs solicited from successful high school and intercollegiate coaches throughout the United States and England. You'll also find a few of our own favorites. The plays, organized in alphabetical order and clearly illustrated, are suitable for all skill levels. However, when selecting plays for teams at the lower skill levels, you may want to choose those that require fewer passes or fewer players.

We have divided this book into three parts. Part I is devoted to free kicks, and we explain the difference between direct and indirect free kicks. You will learn how to deal with various defensive tactics, and you will find 36 free-kick plays and additional variations to help your team overcome those tactics.

Part II, on corner kicks, also lists the applicable rules and describes how to deal with various defensive tactics. The 22 corner-kick plays and variations will be a valuable offensive scoring resource.

Part III features throw-ins and kickoffs. We discuss the relevant rules and ways to counter different defensive tactics. You will find 12 throw-in and 10 kickoff plays—and variations of them—to strengthen your team's play in these situations.

Soccer Restart Plays is unique in that it provides coaches with many restart plays that have withstood the test of time. Devoting significant practice time to restart plays seems not only logical but essential. Expect using this book to pay off in goals.

Acknowledgments

We are grateful to the coaches who contributed to *Soccer Restart Plays* and to Kenneth Simon, a former outstanding soccer player at Glassboro State College (now Rowan University), who suggested the need for such a book. We also thank Cliff McCrath, head coach at Seattle Pacific University, and Jerry Yeagley, head coach at Indiana University, the 1998 NCAA Division I Men's National Champions, valued contributors to our books, for their endorsements. It has been our pleasure to work with Human Kinetics publishers on our six books. In particular, we thank Brian Holding for his guidance on our earlier books, Mary Fowler for her advice on the first edition of this book, and Jeff Riley and Melinda Graham for their astute recommendations and friendly assistance on this book.

Play Finder

FREE KICKS

CORNER KICKS

CORNER KICKS

THROW-INS AND KICKOFFS

Paul Martinez/PHOTOSPORT

PART I

THE FREE KICK

The best place to begin our presentation of restart plays is with a situation that gives the offense a high percentage of kicks that score—the free kick. Gaining a tactical advantage in the free-kick situation takes proper positioning and quick thinking on the part of your offense. One of your biggest coaching challenges is to prepare your players to organize themselves efficiently for free kicks. Whether the shot at goal comes from a single player's direct attempt or involves two or three teammates, all your players need to be ready to execute their roles.

In part I, we discuss free-kick strategy. We give you tips for determining what plays to use in particular situations you may face. Chapter 1 begins by distinguishing between direct and indirect free kicks. We look at defensive tactics your team might encounter and help you assess the defense's strengths and weaknesses by looking at its positioning. To assist you in strategy formation, we provide an overview of attacking tactics you can use when your team is awarded a free kick.

In chapter 2, you'll find 36 free-kick plays used and designed by premier college and high school coaches. Many plays include variations, giving you additional options for attacking the goal. The helpful diagrams that accompany each play show you how to position players and sequence their movements so your team is sure to score! We've included offensive and defensive tips to help you select plays for specific situations.

Remember, in the heat of competition, even experienced players can forget or ignore what they have learned. So have your team practice free kicks repeatedly. Practice the plays first without opposition until the key players learn their roles, then bring in defenders gradually, ending with 11 v 11 game-like situations, and call frequent fouls in varying locations. During the 11 v 11 play, observe and critique the offensive and defensive setups. This practice will increase the players' confidence and make for better execution of restart plays.

Free Kick Tactics

An offense taking a free kick has, percentage-wise, one of soccer's best chances to score. A team takes a free kick to resume play after the referee has stopped the game for certain rule violations. The kick is a penalty for the team that commits the violation.

Rules for the Free Kick

- On a direct free kick, a team may score a goal directly from the initial kick.
- On an indirect free kick, a team may not score a goal directly from the initial kick. A player other than the initial kicker must play or touch the ball before it passes through the goal.
- The free kick is taken from the point where the violation occurred (unless otherwise specified in the rules).
- Defenders cannot be within 10 yards of the ball until it is in play, unless standing on the goal line between the goalposts. If a player on the defending team is within 10 yards of the ball and intentionally interferes with the free kick, the kick is retaken. Any player who tries to slow the game by not getting 10 yards from the ball is first cautioned; if the violation is repeated, the player may be ejected from the game.

- As soon as the ball is in position to be played, the referee gives a signal, usually a whistle. The ball must be stationary for the kick and is not in play until it has traveled the distance of its circumference (27 inches). The kicker may send the ball in any direction—but may not play the ball again until it has been touched or played by another player.
- Whether the free kick is successful depends on a number of factors, particularly the offensive team's ability to execute a set play effectively and exploit any defensive weaknesses. The team executing such tactics as moving quickly on transition, being first to the ball, and getting goal-side usually comes out ahead in competition, so it is essential that the coach devote adequate time to practicing them.

Defensive Tactics

It is essential for a coach to understand general defensive tactics and, even more so, the opponent's specific strengths and weaknesses. This understanding goes into setting up and practicing an effective game plan.

The primary strategy in defending against free kicks is to switch immediately from offense to defense and deny attackers the opportunity to get behind the defense. Players defending against free kicks position themselves according to the location of the ball relative to the goal being attacked. A "wall" is formed, as shown in figure 1.1, with four to five players in the center of the penalty area, three to four at the sides of the penalty area, two to three at the flanks and areas 20 or more yards outside the penalty area, and one or two players elsewhere on the field.

When the attacking team is taking a free kick from the third of the field nearest the opponent's goal, defenders should cover their positions immediately and form a wall of two to five players—or more in a goal-line situation. The primary purpose of the wall is to protect the near-post portion of their goal, which is most vulnerable to a shot on goal from a restart play. The goalkeeper covers the far post and must be able to see the ball. After the goalkeeper indicates how many players are needed in the wall, the goalkeeper or a field player gives instructions for setting the wall. This must be done quickly so that the goalkeeper has time to set up and not get caught

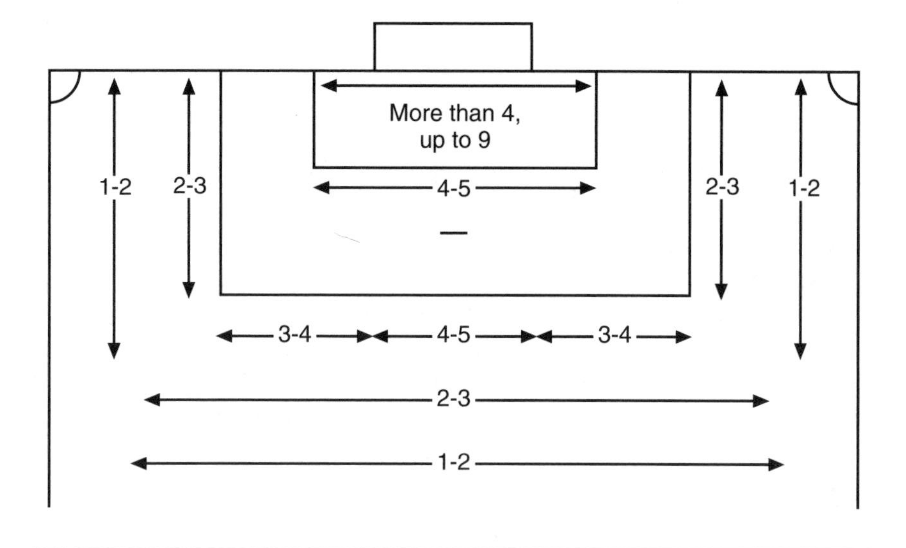

Figure 1.1 The usual number of players in the wall, depending on where the ball is relative to the goal.

out of position by an attacker's quick kick. The goalkeeper or field player sets the wall's first defender in line with the near post and 10 yards from the ball. The first defender, who should be the tallest player, stands still and the other wall players stand to the inside of this player. Too few or too many defenders in the wall can cause numerical disadvantages and expose the goalkeeper to danger. If there are too few defenders in the wall the goalkeeper has too much area to cover to the far post. If there are too many defenders, the goalkeeper has to move nearer to the far post to see the ball, which opens up the near post for a shot over or around the wall at that end. The wall players react to the ball.

On a direct kick, the wall players do not move until the ball is kicked, and must not duck or turn when the ball is hit at them. In the World Cup '98 game between Colombia and England, two of Colombia's wall players ducked as David Beckham's direct shot swerved over them for England's second goal in the 2-0 win to advance to the second round.

On an indirect kick, once the first pass is made, defenders must pressure the player with the ball. Defenders not in the wall closely mark attackers in key areas. Once the free kick has been taken and attacking from the field ensues, defenders move to challenge attackers, never letting one settle on the ball. After the ball is cleared, all defenders move out of the defensive area and go on attack immediately.

A wall is not set up for free kicks not in the attacking third of the field. The focus here is for the team conceding the ball to quickly threaten the free kick from 10 yards and mark players and space. Defenders generally position themselves between their goal and the attackers they are marking. They closely mark the attacker with the ball and others nearby. Defenders need not mark attackers in extreme positions tightly; they are farther from the ball, and there will be time to make adjustments when the kick is taken. Marking becomes tighter for free kicks in the middle third of the field. Regardless of the position of the ball when a foul is called, all defenders must get into position immediately to prevent a quick attack on goal.

Attacking Tactics

On free kicks the attacking team enjoys significant advantages:

- The team has possession of a stationary ball.
- No opponent may be within 10 yards of the ball until it is kicked.
- The offense may act quickly and score a goal while the defenders are adjusting to the situation. Conversely, they have time to execute a well-practiced set play.
- A high percentage of goals are scored from free kicks.

These advantages, in addition to effective utilization of the attackers' strengths and exploitation of the defenders' weaknesses, are parts of the puzzle the coach must put together in the game plan. Pregame scouting will provide the coach with information to help determine what restart plays might be effective. These plays must be part of a team's practice sessions prior to a game. Additional information gained during the game can be passed along to the team via substitutions and in the coach's halftime instructions to the players.

A coach should watch the opponent's defense. Specific details to be aware of include

- how fast the players move in transition from attack to defense;
- who sets the wall and how quickly;
- whether they "cheat" in setting the wall (i.e., set up nearer than 10 yards from the ball);

- how well they set up the wall (number of players in the wall, open space at the near post end, whether the goalkeeper can see the ball);
- whether the wall players follow up quickly after a shot on goal;
- the height and heading ability of the defenders;
- the aggressiveness and jumping ability of the goalkeeper;
- how the goalkeeper handles high or low balls; and
- whether the goalkeeper punches or tries to catch difficult balls.

When your team is awarded a free kick, the first priority is to act quickly to exploit defensive weaknesses. Free kicks in the midfield or defensive area of the field should be taken quickly to catch the defense in transition confusion. In Argentina's second round World Cup '98 game with England, a quick return on a free kick from the defensive goal area almost cost England dearly as Argentina's attack resulted in a shot on goal. If the foul calls for a direct kick in the attacking third of the field and the defense is slow in setting the wall, a quick direct shot on goal has a reasonable chance of resulting in a score.

If the defense sets up quickly, the coach or a designated attacker signals—by word or physical action—which restart play to execute. Some teams "cheat" and set the wall closer than 10 yards from the ball on the assumption this will be to their advantage if the referee permits it, or will slow down play if the referee moves the wall back. This ploy could backfire if the wall is moved back because it will change the angle of coverage and may expose open area for the attackers to exploit. The attacking team should ask for the 10 yards if it cannot take a quick shot on goal.

Even though only one, two, or three attackers usually touch the ball on a restart play, all have roles, with some of them serving as decoys. The timing of these decoy runs is important, as they pull defenders away from the space needed for the play. England's defenders followed decoy runs by Argentine attackers and left another attacker open behind the defensive wall. The unmarked attacker took full advantage of England's defensive lapse by scoring the tying goal with seconds remaining in the first half of their World Cup '98 second round game. The play used by Argentina was similar to the "Open Player on End of Wall" play in chapter 2.

In addition to the defenders' weaknesses, the spot where the ball is to be kicked from and the attackers' strengths will determine the best restart play to use. The less complicated the play, the greater the chance of success, particularly with novice players.

Direct shots or shots from one pass are most effective in the central area. A team with good ball handlers can use quick pass plays, and a team with good headers can use plays that put the ball in the air. A coach fortunate enough to have one or more players with the ability to take accurate "banana" (swerving) or blast shots should use these players on direct kicks or indirect kicks using one pass. An effective play from the central area involves one or more attackers positioning themselves on one or both ends of the defensive wall. These players turn or duck as a swerving or blast shot is taken toward them on the way to either the near or far post. Such shots often beat the goalkeeper, whose view has been temporarily blocked.

Restart plays from the sides of the penalty area and the flank areas should be designed to get the ball behind the defense. Attackers want to get goal-side and be first to the ball. More attackers can be brought in to outnumber the defenders. During the first round of World Cup '98, Yugoslavia capitalized twice on restart plays, winning 1-0 games against Iran and the United States. In the first game, a Yugoslavian player at the near-post end of Iran's wall turned behind the wall as Sinisa Mihajvovic bent a shot through the space vacated and beat the Iranian goalkeeper. Two defensive errors contributed to the Yugoslavian goal as the Iranian player at the near-post end of the wall turned away instead of trying to block the shot, and the Iranian goalkeeper's initial move was to the far post, making it impossible to change direction in time to stop the shot. In the game against the United States, a Yugoslavian attacker took a blistering direct shot to the far post past the U.S. wall. A diving save by U.S. goalkeeper Brad Friedel deflected the shot, but the goal was scored by Yugoslavia's Slobodan Komijenovic, who had gotten behind the U.S. defenders and headed the ball into the goal.

An excellent example of a successful indirect free kick from the side of the penalty area was the deciding goal for England in its World Cup '98 game against Tunisia. After the initial pass, a high ball was delivered to the outside of the Tunisian wall and, at the same time, two English attackers made decoy runs around opposite ends of the wall to open space. England's captain, Alan Shearer, took the ultimate advantage of the open space by beating a Tunisian defender to the high ball and directing the ball into the goal at the far post.

Finally, shots and rebounds must be followed up and defenders challenged until the ball is cleared, after which the attackers must make an immediate transition back to defense.

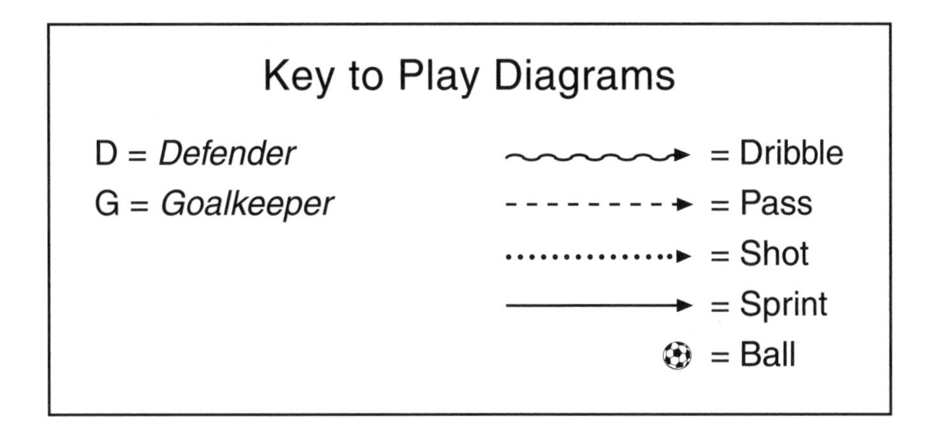

Refer to this key for chapters 2, 4, 6, and 8.

Free Kick Plays

Understanding the tactics and variables involved in free kicks is essential. Your job as coach is to make sure you devote adequate time to practicing them. Practice makes perfect. During practice, your team should thoroughly rehearse a few of the 36 plays that follow, so that play selection, signaling, and execution are precise on game day. Players practicing, intent on improvement, will see their efforts rewarded when they score goals from kick restarts. The coach or a designated field player signals the play to be executed. Play selection is based on these variables:

- whether the free kick is direct or indirect,
- the distance from the goal being attacked,
- the positions taken by the defenders,
- strengths and weaknesses of both attackers and defenders, and
- environmental conditions (wet weather might suggest a hard shot to the goalkeeper, whose hands may be wet or who might slip; wind may prompt keeping the ball on the ground; sun may disturb the vision of the goalkeeper, suggesting a high lofted shot).

As indicated in chapter 1, the likelihood of a free kick's success is enhanced by such tactics as being organized and setting up the play quickly, getting goal-side of the defenders, completing the defensive wall at either or both ends to block the goalkeeper's view, being first to the ball, taking swerving shots or blasting direct shots on goal from the central area, playing the ball to the back of the defense from side and flank areas, and taking the kick quickly in the midfield. Finally, it is essential to PRACTICE, PRACTICE, PRACTICE.

Apple's Delight

Formation

The ball is placed 40 to 50 yards from the goal and slightly to the right of the center circle. Attacker 1 is in position to take the free kick. Attacker 6 is straight ahead of 1, at the top of the penalty area. Attacker 2 is just inside the penalty-area restraining arc, a few yards from 6. Attackers 3, 4, and 5 stand in a line along the left side of the 18-yard line.

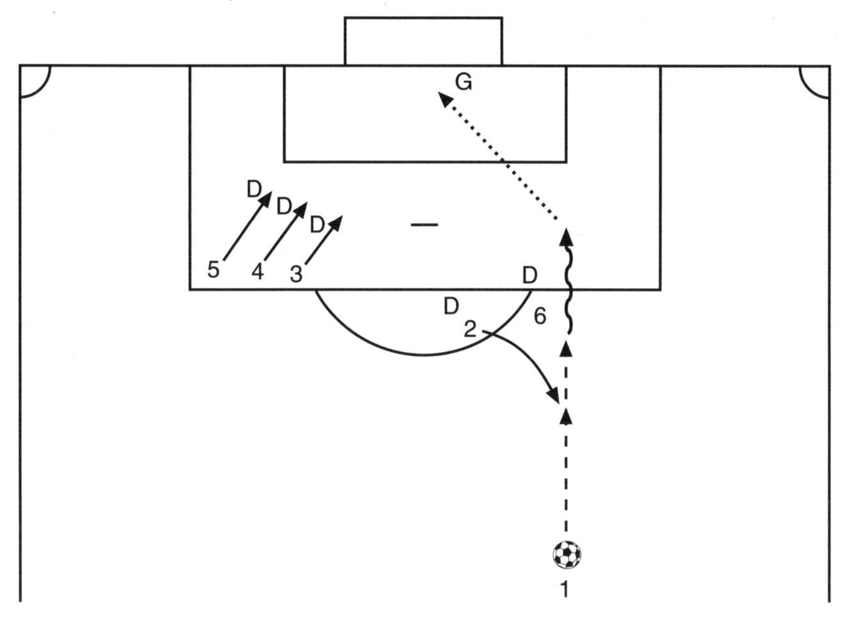

Procedure

Attacker 2 starts the play by moving toward the ball and calling for the pass. 1 makes a crisp pass to 2, who lets the ball run through to 6. 6 shields the ball from the defender, turns with the ball to the outside, and, after one or two touches, takes a shot to the far post. 3, 4, and 5 move to the goal to be in position for a possible rebound. One of these players must cover the far post.

Defensive Tips

Position a defender 10 yards from 1 to challenge the pass. 2's defender should move with the attacker for a possible interception and to prevent a numerical advantage for the attack. Defenders need to stay goal-side of 6 and 3, 4, and 5 to prevent a open shot on goal.

Offensive Tips

If 6 is open, 1 makes the pass as noted. If a defender is threatening the pass, 1 makes a lob pass over the wall to 3, 4, or 5, who must run to get goal-side of the defenders and be first to the ball.

Contributor: Stephen R. Locker, Men's Coach, Harvard University, Cambridge, Massachusetts

Around the Wall

Formation

The ball is placed just outside the right side of the 18-yard line. Attackers 1, 2, and 3 are in position to take the free kick, standing equidistant from the ball to the left, right, and rear, respectively.

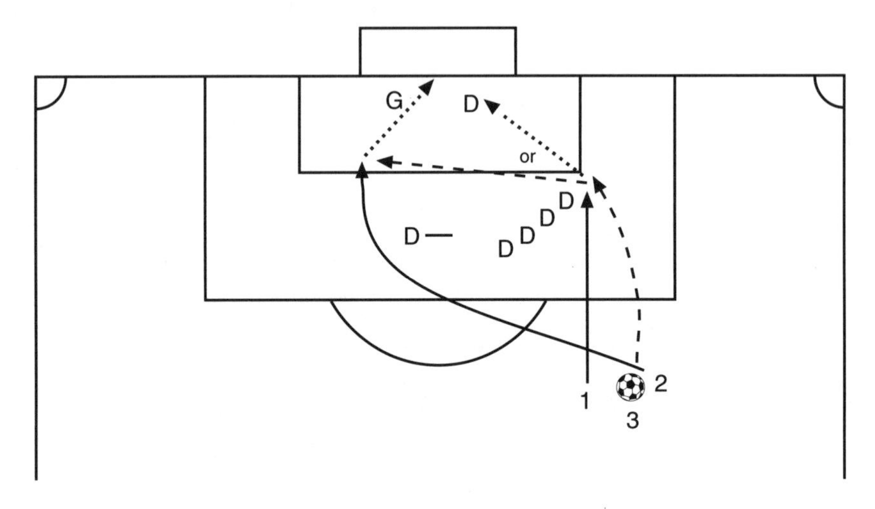

Procedure

1 runs across the ball to the right side of the defensive wall. Almost simultaneously, 2 cuts behind 1 and runs across the ball to the left side of the wall toward the far post. 3 passes to 1, who shoots on goal toward the near post or hooks the ball back to the far post to 2, who shoots on goal.

Defensive Tips

Defenders quickly set a three- or four-player wall 10 yards from the ball with the tallest player at the near-post end. The goalkeeper covers the far post and must be able to see the ball. To prevent breaking up the wall, another defender picks up 2.

Offensive Tips

If, on a direct kick, the wall is not set quickly or effectively and 3 can see open space at the near post, 3 should take a shot at it. If the defense is set, this is a good play for ball handlers. Timely decoy runs, effective passes, and a quick shot are essential to the success of this play.

Contributor: Manfred Schellscheidt, Men's Coach, Seton Hall University, South Orange, New Jersey

Attacking the Post

Formation

The ball is placed 10 yards outside the middle of the 18-yard line. Attacker 1 is in position to take the free kick. Attacker 2 is five yards to the right of 1, and Attacker 3 is five yards to the right of 2.

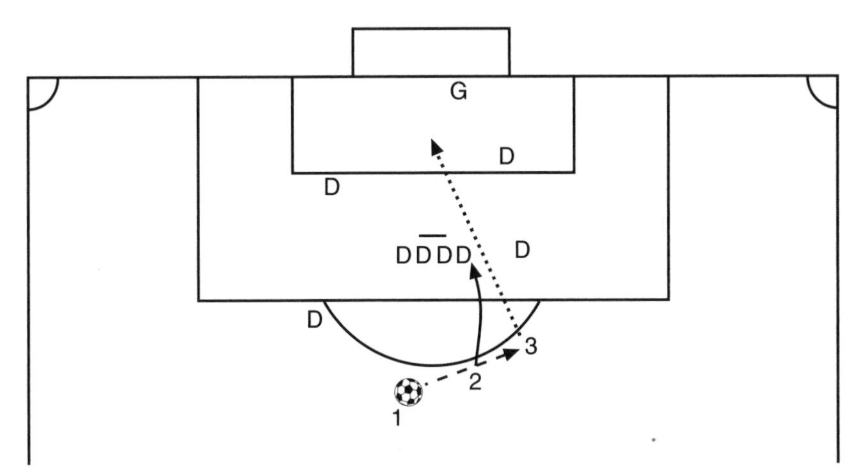

Procedure

2 runs toward the near-post end of the defensive wall. 1 passes to 3, who takes a first-time shot on goal.

Variation 1

2 runs toward the near-post end of the defensive wall. 1 passes to 3. 3 passes to 2, who takes a first-time shot on goal or controls the ball and then takes a shot on goal.

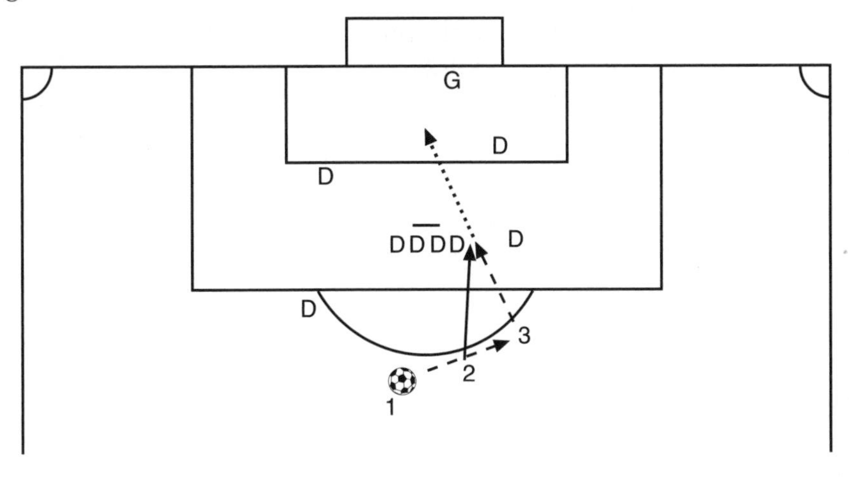

continued

Attacking the Post *(continued)*

Variation 2

2 runs toward the near-post end of the defensive wall. 1 passes to 3. 3 passes to 2. 3 follows up the pass, receives a square pass from 2, and either takes a first-time shot on goal or controls the ball and takes a shot on goal.

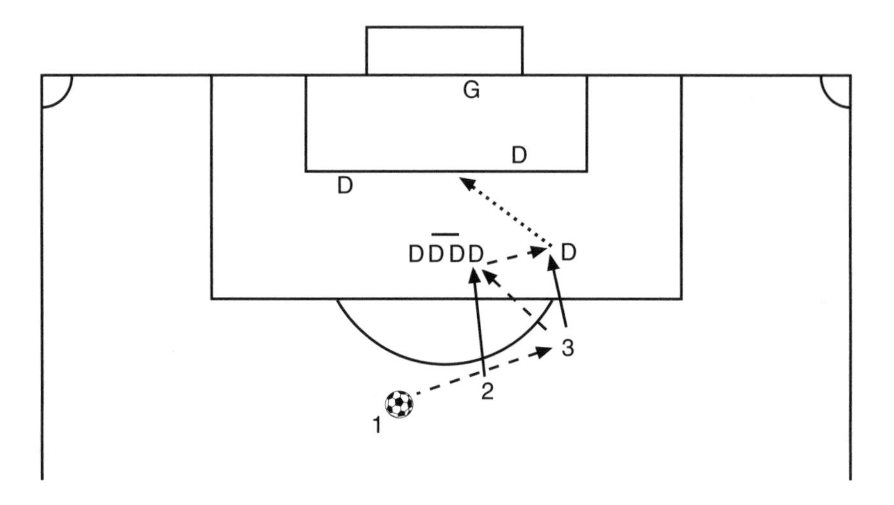

Defensive Tips

Defenders quickly set a four- to five-player wall with the tallest player at the near-post end. The goalkeeper covers the far post and must be able to see the ball. If a pass is made, the wall players move quickly to pressure the ball.

Offensive Tips

If the kicker can see open space on a direct free kick, a first-time shot should be taken. 2 can run to the end of the wall and 1 can take a swerving shot around or over 2, who ducks or moves behind the wall as the shot is taken. Variation 2 should be attempted only by advanced players with good ball-handling skills.

Contributor: Gus Constantine, Men's Coach, New York Institute of Technology, Old Westbury, New York

Back Door the Wall

Formation

The ball is placed just outside the right corner of the penalty area. Attackers 1 and 2 are in position to take the free kick. Attacker 3 takes a weak-side position even with the defensive wall and about 20 yards to the side of it.

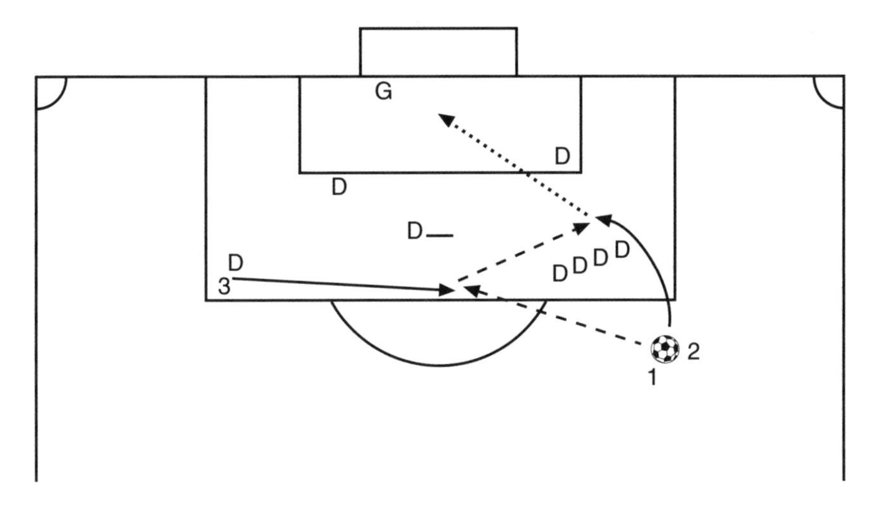

Procedure

1 fakes a shot on goal and runs over the ball around the near-post side of the wall, staying onside. In rapid sequence, 2 passes to 3, who has made a timed run toward the wall, and 3 makes a one-touch pass behind the wall to 1, who takes a shot on goal.

Defensive Tips

Defenders quickly set up a three- to four-player wall with the tallest player at the near-post end. The goalkeeper covers the far post and must be able to see the ball.

Offensive Tips

If 1 or 2 can see open space, either can take a first-time shot on a direct kick. If 3 has a clear shot or if 1 is covered, 3 can take a shot to the near post.

Contributor: Jerry Yeagley, Men's Coach, Indiana University, Bloomington, Indiana

Blast-Off

Formation

The ball is placed just outside the midpoint of the penalty-area restraining arc. Attackers 1 and 2 are in position to take the free kick. Attacker 3 stands slightly in front of the left end of the defensive wall. Attacker 4 is five yards to the right of 1. Attackers 5 and 6 are 10 yards to the left and right, respectively, of the defensive wall.

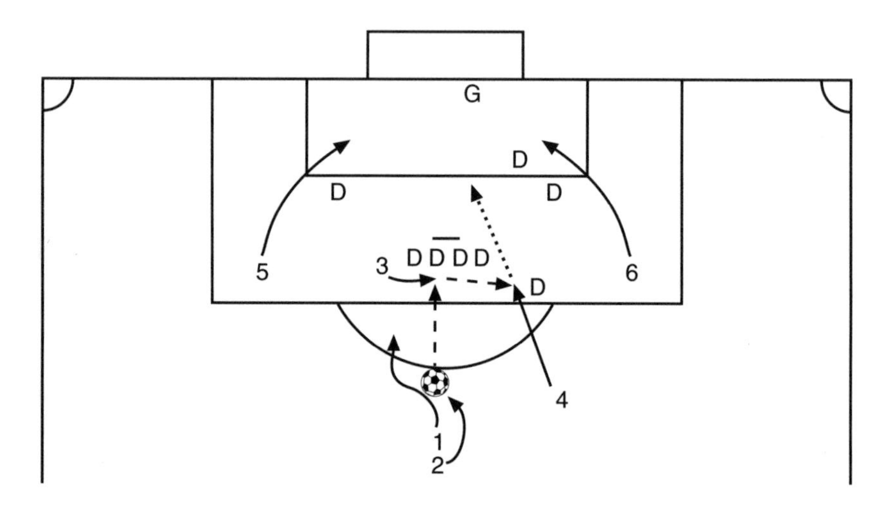

Procedure

1 runs as if to take a blast shot on goal but instead runs over the ball and off to the left. 2 follows 1 and takes a low, hard shot toward the defensive wall. 3, moving across in front of the wall, taps the ball to 4, who, after a momentary delay, moves to receive the pass and take a first-time shot on goal. 5 and 6 move to the post areas to stay alert for a possible rebound.

Defensive Tips

Defenders quickly set up a four- to five-player wall with the tallest player at the near-post end. The goalkeeper covers the far post and must be able to see the ball.

Offensive Tips

If, on a direct free kick, 1 or 2 can see space at the near post, either can take a shot on goal toward 3, who ducks or turns behind the wall.

Contributor: J. Malcolm Simon, Professor and Director Emeritus of Physical Education and Athletics, New Jersey Institute of Technology, Newark, New Jersey

Boyler Options

Formation

The ball is placed 10 yards outside the right side of the 18-yard line. Attackers 1, 2, and 3 are in position to take the free kick. Attackers 4, 5, and 6 are in a line along the far left side of the 18-yard line. Attacker 7 stands at the near-post end of the defensive wall.

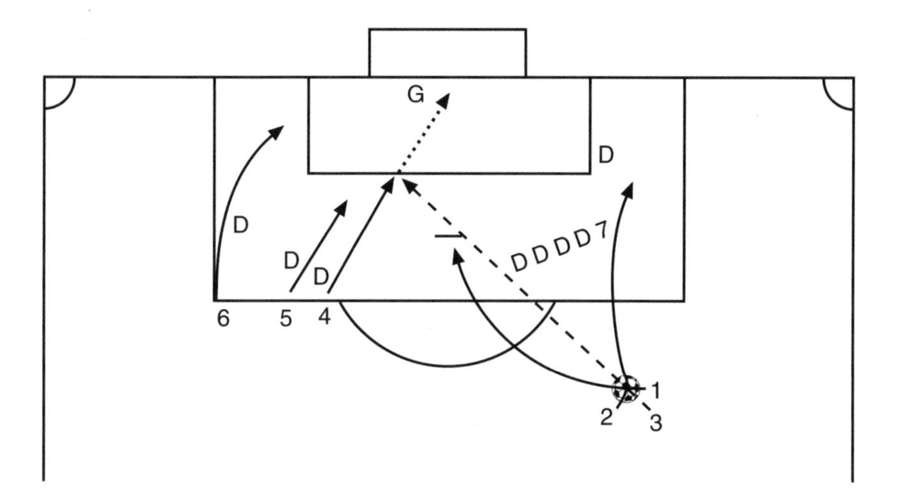

Procedure

In sequence, 1 runs over the ball and makes a curling run toward the penalty line; 2 runs over the ball and makes a straight run past 7 at the near-post end of the wall; 4, 5, and 6 run toward the far post; 3 makes a lob pass to the far post, setting up 4, 5, or 6 for a one-time head shot on goal. The runs and pass must be timed to avoid players off the ball getting into offside positions.

continued

Variation

1 runs over the ball and makes a curling run toward the near post. 2 runs over the ball and makes a straight run past 7 at the near-post end of the defensive wall. 3 makes a ground pass to 2, who passes to 1 at the near post. As 2 passes to 1, Attackers 4, 5, and 6 sprint toward the goal area to be in position for a possible rebound. 1 takes a first-time shot on goal.

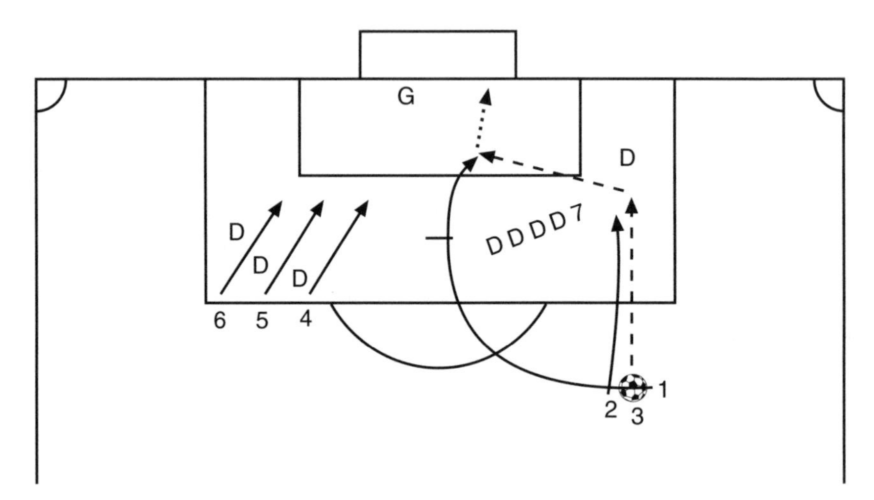

Defensive Tips

Defenders must quickly set a three- to four-player wall with the tallest player at the near-post end. The goalkeeper covers the far post and must see the ball. Those defending against attackers 4, 5, and 6 must not let them get goal-side. The goalkeeper must get to the ball as high as possible in its flight and catch or clear it.

Offensive Tips

4, 5, and 6 must get goal-side and be first to the ball. 1 and 2 follow the play and are alert for rebounds.

Contributor: Gavin Donaldson, Men's Coach, West Virginia Wesleyan College, Buckhannon, West Virginia

Cortland

Formation

The ball is placed 50 yards from the goal line on the left side of the field. Attacker 2 is in position to take the free kick. Attacker 1 is behind and to the left of 2. Attackers 3 and 4 are on the opposite side of the field. Attackers 5, 6, 7, and 8 spread out in the middle of the field as far toward the goal as the defense allows.

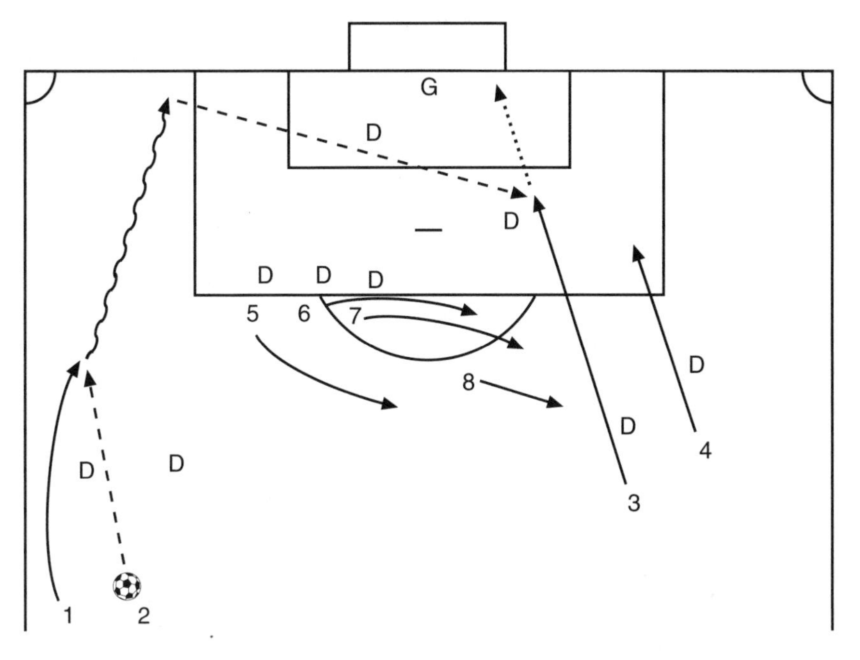

Procedure On a predetermined signal, 5, 6, 7, and 8 move away from the middle of the field to create space for 1, who is overlapping on the left side of the field. 2 passes the ball to 1. 1 takes the ball to the goal line and crosses to 3 and 4, who are sprinting toward the goal. The first player to get the ball shoots on goal. 5, 6, 7, and 8 stay alert for a possible rebound or defensive clear.

Defensive Tips Players move quickly to cover attackers one on one near the ball. Other defenders must be alert to prevent attackers from getting goal-side. Bring defenders back to prevent the attack from gaining a numerical advantage. If 2 beats the defender, another defender must cover to prevent 2 from going on goal or making an easy pass. The first defender cuts to the penalty area to pick up an open player.

Offensive Tips 3 and 4 must make well-timed and aggressive runs to get goal-side of the defense and be first to the ball.

Contributor: Chris J. Malone, Associate Athletic Director, State University of New York College at Cortland, Cortland, New York

Delay

Formation

The ball is placed just outside the midpoint of the penalty-area restraining arc. Attackers 1 and 2 are in position to take the free kick. Attacker 3 is 10 yards to the right and slightly forward of 1. Attacker 4 stands in front of the left end of the defensive wall.

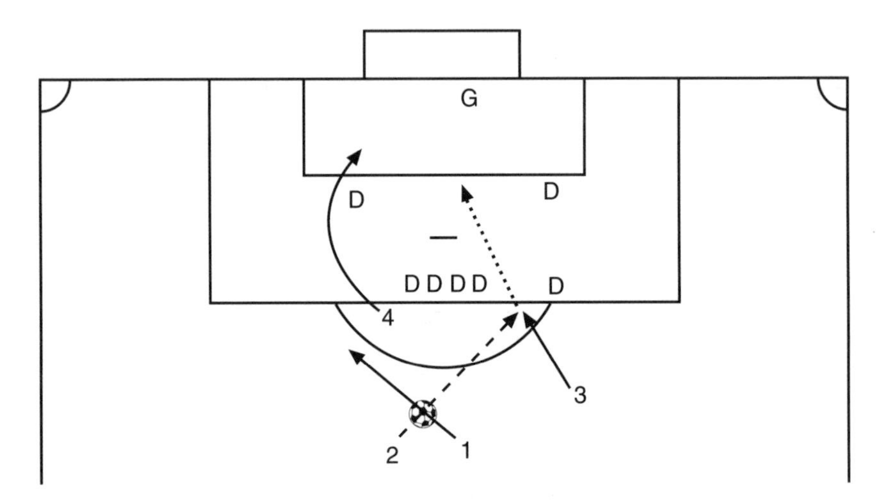

Procedure

1 moves across the ball and off to the left side as 2 follows immediately with a direct pass to 3, who makes a delayed sprint forward to take a first-time shot on goal. 4 spins off the left end of the defensive wall to be ready for a possible rebound.

Defensive Tips

Defenders quickly set up a four- to five-player wall with the tallest player at the near-post end. The goalkeeper covers the far post and must be able to see the ball.

Offensive Tips

If this is a direct free kick and 1 or 2 can see space at either post, a shot on goal can be taken.

Contributor: J. Malcolm Simon, Professor and Director Emeritus of Physical Education and Athletics, New Jersey Institute of Technology, Newark, New Jersey

Directional Decoys

Formation

The ball is placed 10 yards outside the right side of the 18-yard line. Attacker 1 is in position to take the free kick. Attackers 2, 3, and 4 stand in a line directly behind 1. Attackers 5 and 6 stand five yards to the right and left, respectively, of the ball.

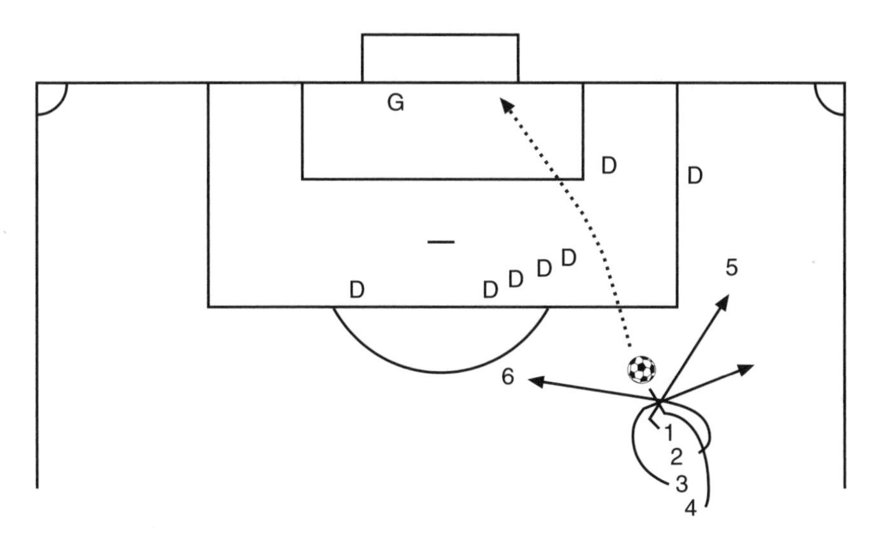

Procedure

The kick is a direct shot on goal around the near end of the wall. The shooter is the player in line designated by an on-field decision of the four players or by a number or letter signal called out by the coach. The nonshooters each run over the ball and break alternately to the left and right of the defensive wall. The direction of the shot will be determined by the setup of the wall and the position of the goalkeeper.

continued

Variation

Instead of taking a shot on goal, the designated player passes to 5, who runs toward the ball to receive the pass. 5 either takes a first-time shot on goal or dribbles into a better position and then takes a shot on goal. 6 runs toward the goal to be in position for a possible rebound.

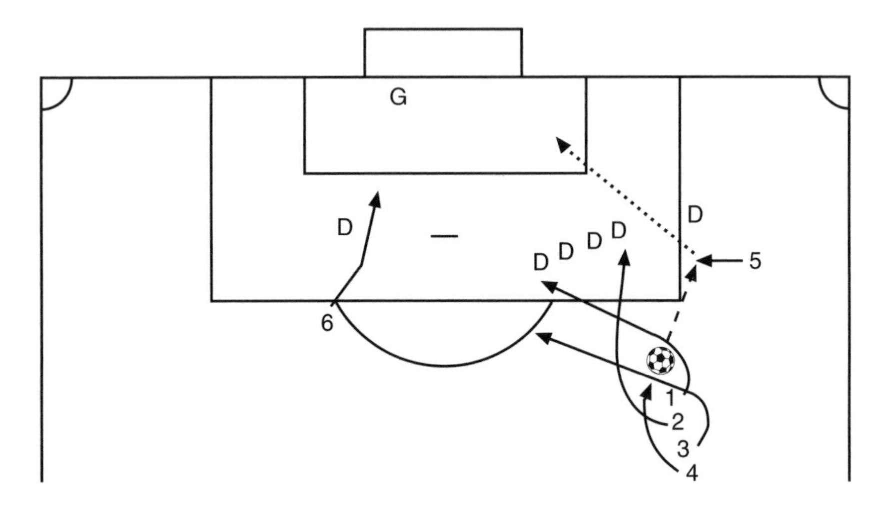

Defensive Tips

Defenders quickly set up a three- to four-player wall with the tallest player at the near-post end. The goalkeeper covers the far post and must be able to see the ball. Defenders not in the wall must not let attackers get goal-side.

Offensive Tips

If the wall is not set quickly, 1 can take a quick shot on goal. If the wall is set and the first players in the attacking line are making decoy runs, the player taking the shot times it so the attackers can stop at the ends of the defensive wall to block the goalkeeper's view, then duck or turn behind the wall on the shot. All attackers stay alert for rebounds.

Contributor: Daniel R. Coombs, Boys' Coach, Loyola Academy, Wilmette, Illinois; Girls' Coach, Mother McAuley High School, Chicago, Illinois

Down the Line

Formation

The ball is placed on either side of the field 20 yards outside the penalty box. Attackers 1 and 2 are in position to take the free kick. Attackers 3, 4, and 5 stand in an arc across the far side of the penalty area. Attacker 6 stands outside the far sideline of the penalty area.

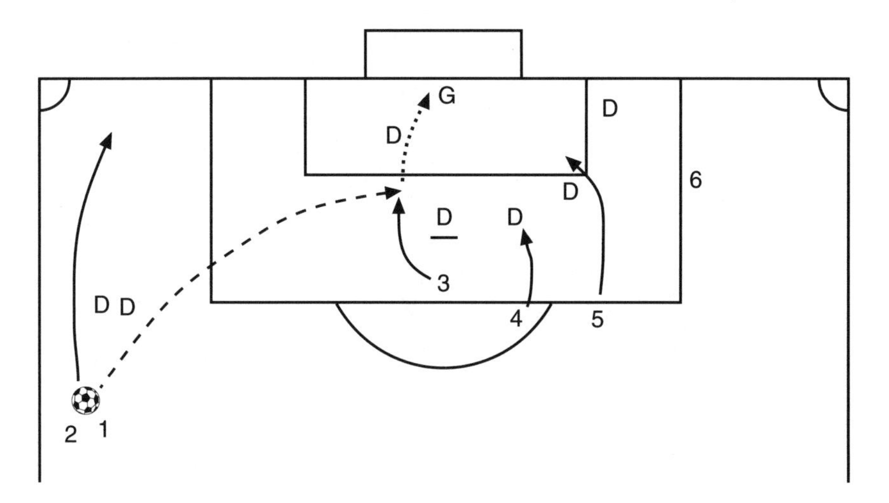

Procedure

1 runs over the ball and continues down the line. 2 passes the ball into the penalty area. On the pass, 3, 4, and 5 make diagonal runs into the penalty area toward the direction of the pass. The first player to touch the ball takes a first-time shot on goal while the other players keep alert for a possible rebound or pass. 6 stays outside the penalty area, alert for a long rebound or attempted clear by the defense.

continued

Variation

1 runs over the ball and continues down the line. 2 passes down the line to 1. 1 makes a first-time pass to the goal area or dribbles the ball to the goal line and passes to either the near or far post. 3, 4, and 5 make timed runs toward the direction of either pass. The first player to touch the ball takes a first-time shot on goal while the other players keep alert for a possible rebound or pass. 6 stays outside the penalty area, alert for a long rebound or attempted clear.

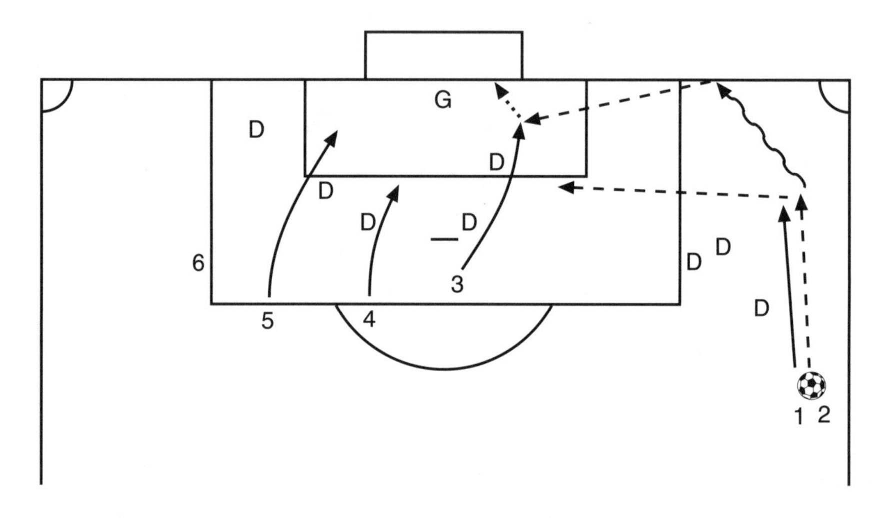

Defensive Tips

Defenders move quickly to cover attackers one on one near the ball. Other defenders work to prevent attackers from getting goal-side. More defenders may have to come back to prevent the attack from gaining a numerical advantage. The goalkeeper must get to the ball as high as possible and clear it or catch it.

Offensive Tips

Attackers must move aggressively to get goal-side and be first to the ball. Directing the shot on goal to either post is more important than a power shot.

Contributor: Alan R. Kirkup, Former Women's Coach, Southern Methodist University, Dallas, Texas

Either Or

Formation

The ball is placed 10 yards outside the midpoint of the penalty-area restraining arc. Attacker 1 is in position to take the free kick. Attacker 2 stands in front of the middle of the defensive wall. Attacker 3 is 10 yards to the right of 1 and halfway between 1 and 2.

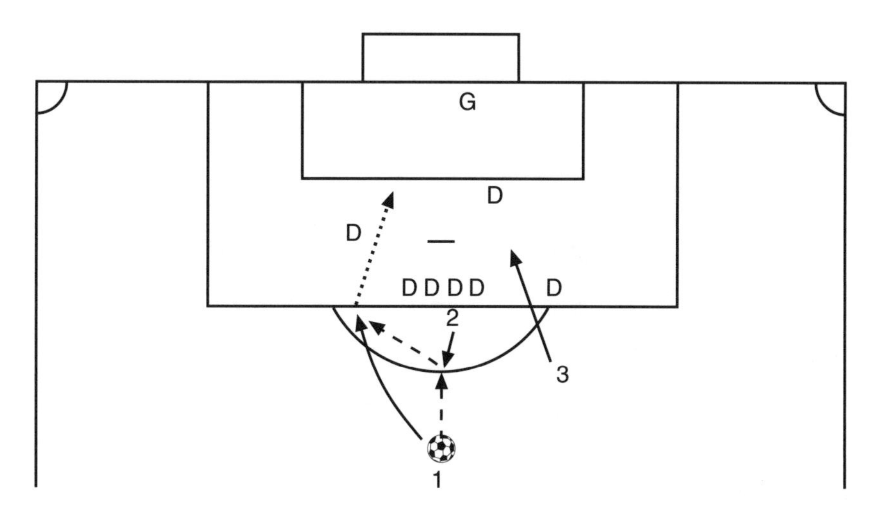

Procedure

As 1 moves to take the kick, 2 moves toward the ball. 1 passes forward to 2. After the pass, 1 immediately moves to the left and receives a pass back from 2. 1 takes a first-time shot on goal. 3 moves to the post to be alert for a possible rebound. If defensive attention is concentrated on 1 and 2, 1 makes a diagonal pass to 3, who moves to the post and takes a first-time shot on goal.

Defensive Tips

Defenders quickly set up a four- to five-player wall with the tallest player at the near-post end. The goalkeeper covers the far post and must be able to see the ball.

Offensive Tips

If the wall is not set quickly, or if the wall is set and 1 can see space at either post, 1 can take a blast or swerving shot.

Contributor: J. Malcolm Simon, Professor and Director Emeritus of Physical Education and Athletics, New Jersey Institute of Technology, Newark, New Jersey

Fake and Chip

Formation

The ball is placed five yards outside the left side of the penalty area. Attackers 1 and 2 are in position to take the free kick to the right and left of the ball, respectively. Attackers 3, 4, and 5 are a few feet apart from each other outside the right side of the penalty area.

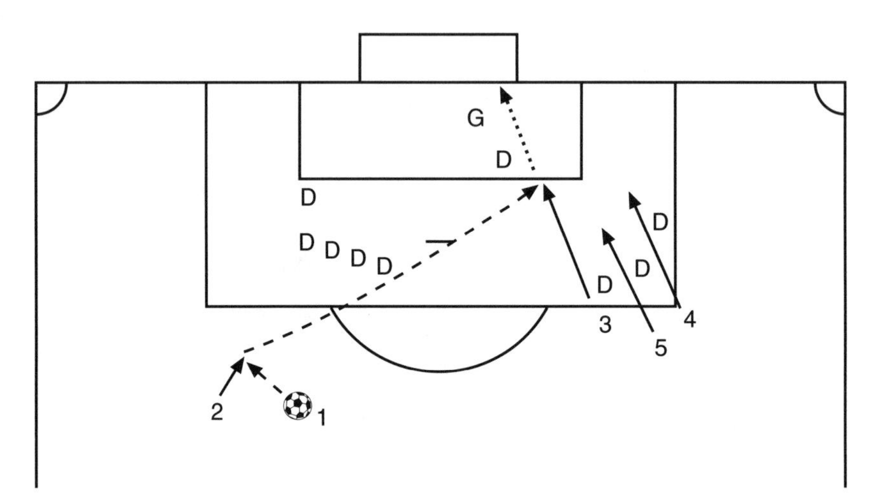

Procedure

The ball is played from 1 to 2 as if for a shot by 2 around the wall. Instead, 2 chips the ball to the far post for 3, 4, and 5, who are simultaneously running toward the goal. Whoever gets the ball takes a first-time shot on goal, and the other players continue toward the goal to be in position for a possible rebound.

Defensive Tips

Defenders quickly set a three- to four-player wall with the tallest player at the near-post end. The goalkeeper covers the far post and must be able to see the ball. Players defending against 3, 4, and 5 must not let them get goal-side. The goalkeeper must play the ball as high as possible and clear it or catch it.

Offensive Tips

3, 4, and 5 must make aggressive runs to get goal-side of the defenders and be first to the ball. Directing the shot to the near or far post is more important than a power shot. The attackers must follow a shot on goal and be alert for rebounds.

Contributor: Mike Getman, Men's Coach, University of Alabama at Birmingham, Birmingham, Alabama

Ghost Behind the Wall

Formation

The ball is placed just outside the midpoint of the penalty-area restraining arc. Attacker 1 stands with a foot on the ball, facing attacker 2, who stands one yard behind the ball. Attackers 3 and 4 stand 15 yards to the right and left, respectively, of the ball.

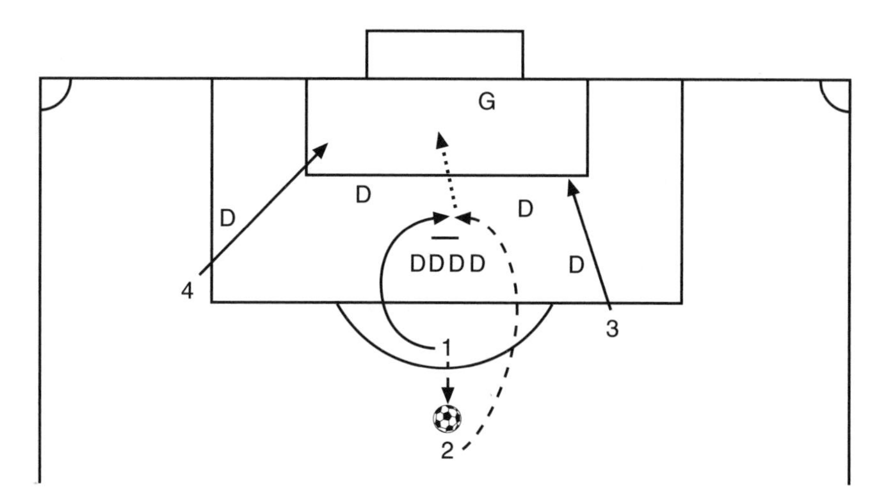

Procedure

On a prearranged signal, 1 rolls the ball to 2. Immediately after this pass, 1 makes a curling run around the wall. 2 makes a chip pass over the wall for 1 to control and shoot on goal. 3 and 4 make timed runs to the post areas to be in position for a possible rebound.

continued

Ghost Behind the Wall *(continued)*

Variation

On a prearranged signal, 1 rolls the ball back to 2. Immediately after this pass, 1 makes a curling run around the wall. 2 makes a chip pass over the wall for 1 to control. 1 passes to either 3 or 4, who shoots on goal.

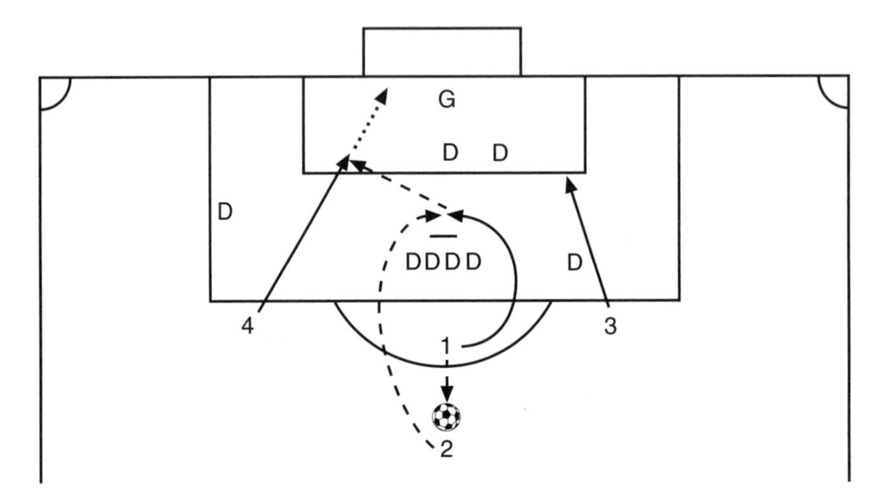

Defensive Tips

Defenders quickly set a four- to five-player wall with the tallest player at the near-post end. The goalkeeper covers the far post and must be able to see the ball. Defenders not in the wall must not let attackers get goal-side or be unmarked in key space near the goal.

Offensive Tips

If 2 sees open space at either post, a direct shot can be taken. 3 and 4 must make aggressive runs to get goal-side and be first to the ball. Directing a shot to either post is more important than power.

Contributor: Stephen G. Scullion, Boys' Coach, Folling Community Club, Pynce and Wear, England

Go Away

Formation

The ball is placed five yards outside the left side of the penalty area. Attackers 1 and 2 are in position to take the free kick. Attacker 3 stands a few yards in front of the right side of the defensive wall. Attackers 5 and 6 stand a few yards apart, just outside the right corner of the goal area. Attacker 4 stands outside the penalty area near the goal line on the right side of the field.

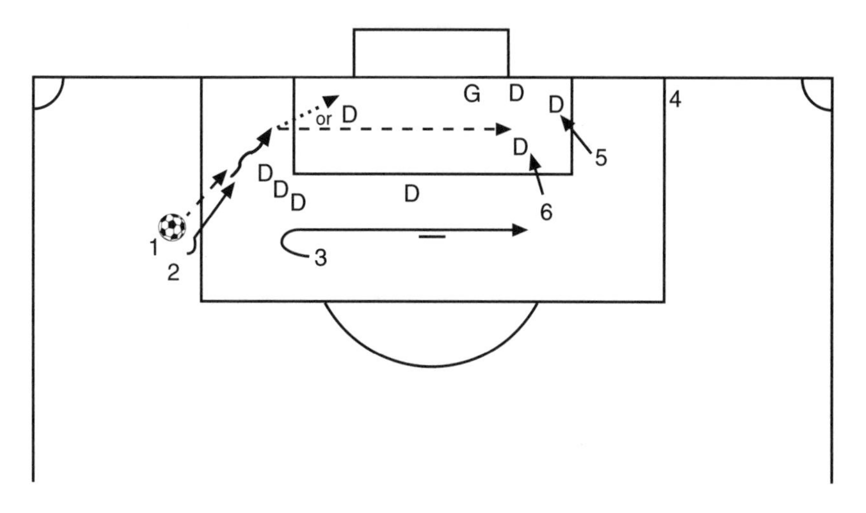

Procedure

3 starts to move toward the ball and is waved away from the play by 1. 3 turns and moves toward 6. 2 runs over the ball and continues toward the near-post end of the defensive wall. 1 steps as if to make a chip pass over the wall but instead passes on the ground to 2, who shields and dribbles the ball around the wall, then either shoots on goal or passes toward the far post to 5 and 6. Whoever gets the ball shoots on goal.

Defensive Tips

Defenders quickly set a two- to three-player wall with the tallest player at the near-post end. The goalkeeper covers the far post and must be able to see the ball. Those players defending against 5 and 6 prevent them from getting goal-side. A defender not in the wall covers 3 to prevent a numerical advantage for the attack.

Offensive Tips

On a direct kick, when the defense sets the wall slowly or poorly and space can be seen at either post, 2 can take a shot on goal. 5 and 6 make aggressive runs to get goal-side and be first to the ball.

Contributor: Harry S. Fleishman, Boys' Coach, Shady Side Academy, Pittsburgh, Pennsylvania

Going for Goal

Formation

The ball is placed 30 yards from the goal line just to the left of the penalty-area restraining arc. Attackers 2 and 3 are in position to take the free kick. Attacker 4 stands about five yards to the right of the ball and about five yards in front of the defensive wall. Attacker 1 stands five yards in front of and to the left of the ball.

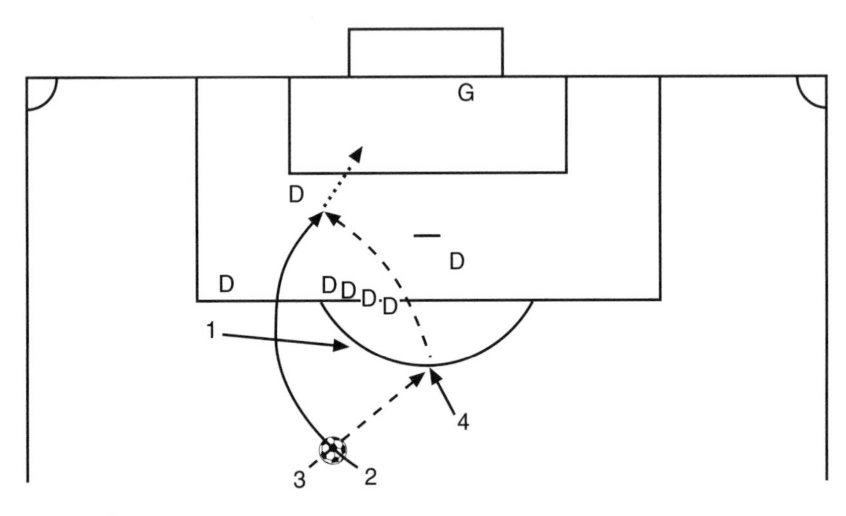

Procedure

1 sprints toward the middle of the field, parallel to the 18-yard line. 2 sprints over the ball toward the area vacated by 1 and continues past the near-post end of the defensive wall. 3 passes the ball to 4, who makes a one-touch pass to 2. 2 shoots on goal.

Defensive Tips

Defenders must quickly set a four- to five-player wall with the tallest player at the near-post end. The goalkeeper covers the far post and must be able to see the ball. A defender not in the wall works to prevent 2 from getting goal-side or being unmarked in a key central scoring area. As soon as the first pass is made, wall defenders move to put pressure on the player with the ball and cover nearby attackers.

Offensive Tips

Good ball handling and well-timed runs are essential for this play. On a direct free kick, 2 can shoot to the near post if space is open. 4 can also shoot on goal if space is open.

Contributor: Gene Chyzowych, Boys' Coach, Columbia High School, Maplewood, New Jersey

Heel

Formation

The ball is placed two yards outside the midpoint of the 18-yard line. Attacker 3 is in position to take the free kick. Attacker 2 stands about 3 yards to the left of 3. Attacker 1 stands about two yards to the right of 3 with attacker 4 about two yards farther to the right. Attacker 5 stands at the right end of the defensive wall. Attacker 6 stands just outside the right side of the penalty area.

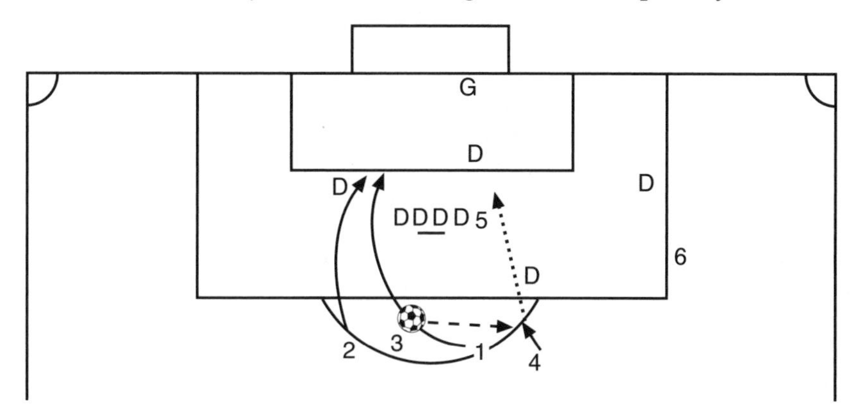

Procedure

1 sprints over the ball toward the near-post end of the defensive wall. 2 sprints around 1. 3, after faking to 1 and 2, heels the ball to 4 who takes a first-time shot on goal. 1 and 2 sprint toward the goal to be in position for a possible rebound.

Variation 1

Following the initial sprints off the ball by 1 and 2, 3 passes to the outside of 5, who turns and shoots on goal. 1, 2, and 6 sprint toward the goal to be in position for a possible rebound.

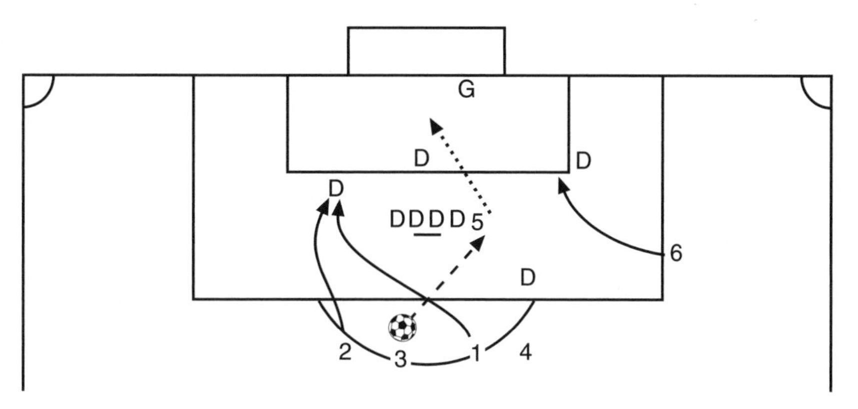

continued

Variation 2

Following the initial sprints off the ball by 1 and 2, 3 makes a chip pass to 6, who has sprinted toward the goal area. 6 takes a first-time shot on goal or passes across the goal to 1 and 2, who have sprinted toward the goal area. Whoever gets the ball shoots on goal.

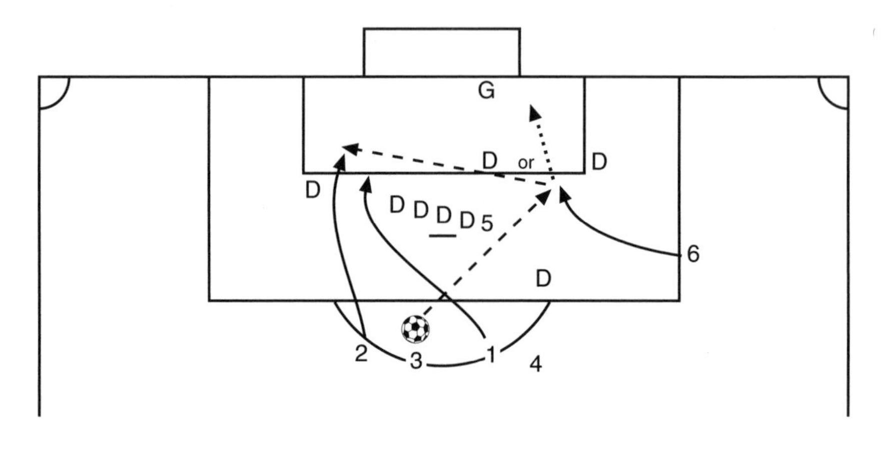

Defensive Tips

Defenders immediately set a four- to five-player wall with the tallest player at the near-post end. The goalkeeper covers the far post and must be able to see the ball.

Offensive Tips

Since excellent ball handling skills and well-timed decoy runs are essential for the success of this play, it is not recommended for novice teams. On a direct free kick, 3 can shoot on goal if space is open.

Contributor: Wayne A. Mones, Men's Coach, Western Connecticut State University, Danbury, Connecticut

Hidden Player

Formation

The ball is placed 20 yards outside the left side of the 18-yard line. Attackers 1, 2, and 3 are in position to take the free kick. Attacker 4 stands in front of the defensive wall. Attacker 5 stands on the right side of the field, square with the ball.

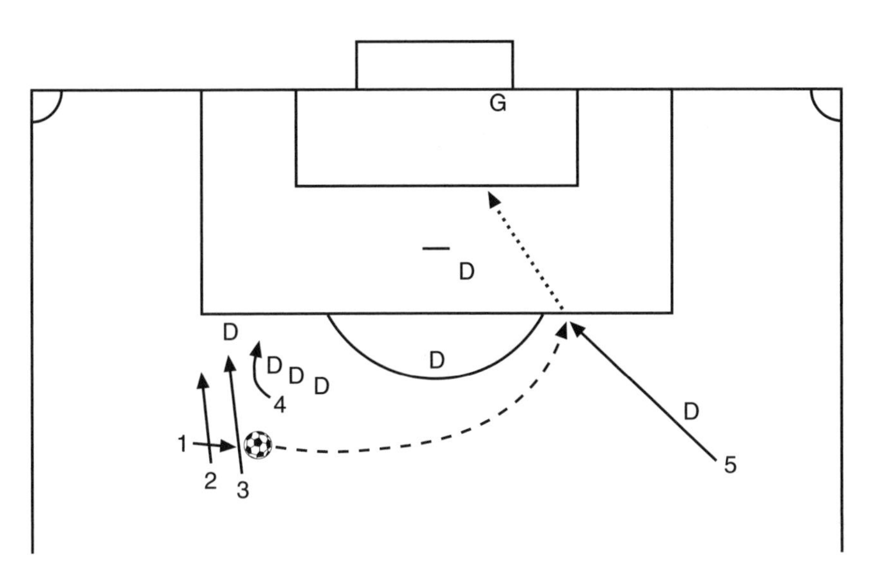

Procedure

2 and 3 sprint explosively toward the left side of the defensive wall. 4 moves to the near-post end of the defensive wall. 1 strikes the ball toward the right side of the penalty area to 5, who has cut inside the defender and run toward the 18-yard line. 5 takes a first-time shot on goal.

Defensive Tips

Defenders quickly set a two- to three-player wall with the tallest player at the near-post end. The goalkeeper covers the far post and must be able to see the ball. Players not in the wall cover 2, 3, 4, and 5 to prevent them from getting goal-side.

Offensive Tips

5, the "hidden player," must be deceptive, fast, and a solid kicker. The timing of 5's run to receive 1's pass is critical. 2, 3, and 4 follow up the play for rebounds.

Contributor: Raul A. Donoso, Boys' Coach, Irvington High School, Irvington, New Jersey

Hot Foot

Formation

The ball is placed inside the left side of the penalty area, 15 yards from the goal line. Attacker 1 stands to the left of the ball in position to take the free kick. Attacker 2 is one yard behind and to the right of the ball. Attacker 3 stands on the midpoint of the penalty-area restraining arc.

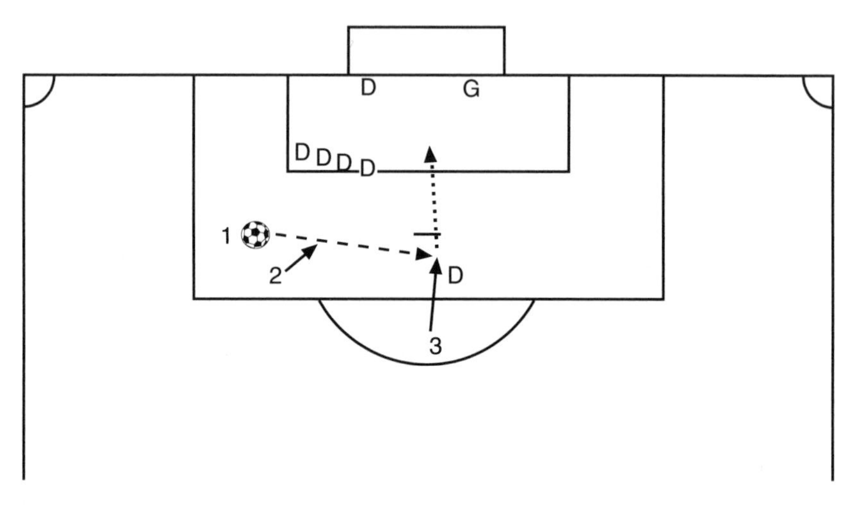

Procedure

2 runs diagonally forward. 1 passes to 2 as 3 simultaneously runs forward. 2 lets the ball run through to 3, who either takes a first-time shot on goal or dribbles to evade a defender and then shoots on goal.

Defensive Tips

Defenders must quickly set a wall. More than four to five players may be needed because the spot of the foul is so close to the goal. The goalkeeper covers the far post and must be able to see the ball.

Offensive Tips

This is an indirect free kick since it is inside the penalty area (a direct free kick would be a penalty kick). If the attacking team is losing and time is running out, more attackers come up to put pressure on the defense.

Contributor: Nick Kvasic, Men's Coach, College of Staten Island, Staten Island, New York

Indirect Screen

Formation

The ball is placed 10 yards outside the middle of the 18-yard line. Attackers 4 and 5 are in position to take the free kick, with 5 facing the defensive wall and 4 standing to the left of and facing the ball. Attackers 2 and 3, both facing the ball, stand close together between the ball and the defensive wall to obstruct the defenders' view of the ball. Attacker 1 stands at the right end of the wall. Attackers 6 and 7 stand at the top of the right side of the 18-yard line.

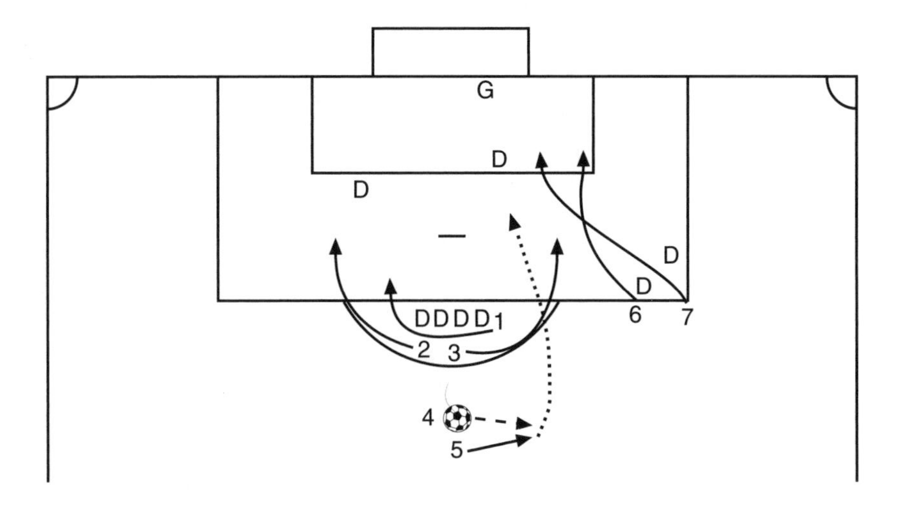

Procedure

1 initiates the play by running across the front of the defensive wall and breaking toward the near post. 4 makes a push pass sideways for 5, who has timed a run to take a one-touch swerving shot on goal around the end of the wall vacated by 1. To be in position for a possible rebound, 6 runs toward the far post, 7 runs toward the goalkeeper, and 2 and 3 break opposite each other and run toward the goal.

continued

Indirect Screen *(continued)*

Variation

1 initiates the play by running across the front of the defensive wall and breaking toward the near post. If the wall is poorly set up, 4 runs over the ball and 5 takes a direct shot on goal. To be in position for a possible rebound, 6 runs toward the far post, 7 runs toward the goalkeeper, and 2 and 3 break opposite each other and run toward the goal.

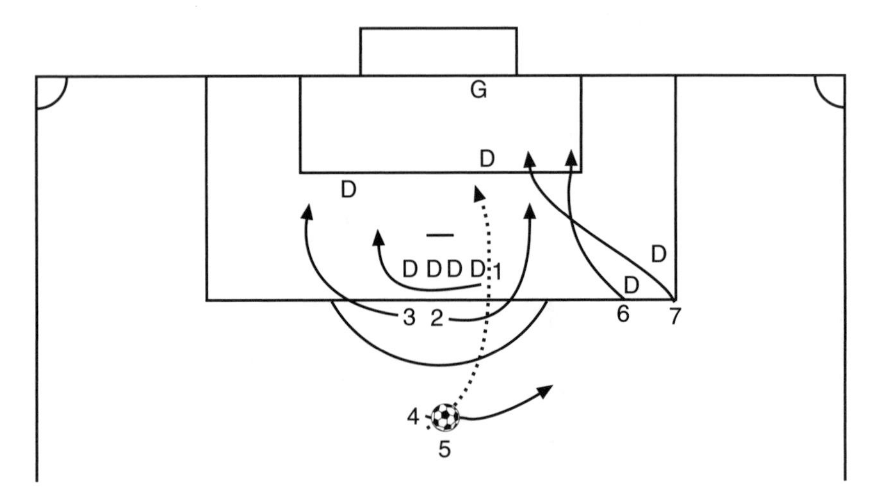

Defensive Tips

Defenders must quickly set a four- to five-player wall with the tallest player at the near-post end. The goalkeeper covers the far post and must be able to see the ball. Players not in the wall cover 6 and 7 to prevent them from getting goal-side. When the pass is made, wall players break quickly to pressure the ball and cover attackers.

Offensive Tips

4 and 5 must disguise their pass-and-run for this play to be effective. 6 and 7 make aggressive runs to get goal-side and be first to the ball. All attackers stay alert for rebounds.

Contributor: Michelle C. Morgan, Women's Coach, Amherst College, Amherst, Massachusetts

Liner Combo

Formation

The ball is placed 10 yards outside the right side of the 18-yard line. Attacker 2 is in position to take the free kick. Attacker 3 stands directly behind 2. Attacker 1 is at the end of the near-post side of the defensive wall. Attacker 4 is 10 yards outside the left side of the 18-yard line.

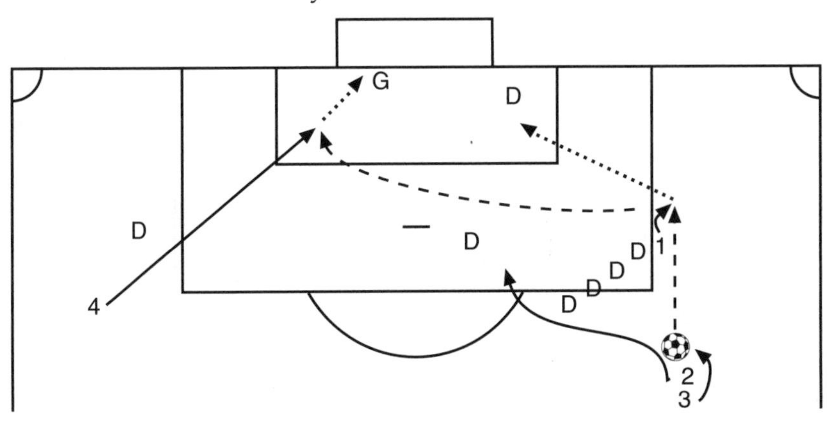

Procedure

2 runs over the ball and past the far-post side of the defensive wall. 3 passes the ball straight down the line to the outside of 1. 1 turns just as the ball passes by and either takes a shot on goal or crosses to 4, who has made a timed run to the far post to be in position for a possible pass and first-time shot on goal.

Variation 1

2 runs over the ball and past the far-post side of the defensive wall. 3 passes to the outside of 2, who makes a one-touch wall pass behind the defensive wall to 1. 1 shoots on goal or crosses to 4, who has made a timed run to the far post to be in position for a possible pass and first-time shot on goal.

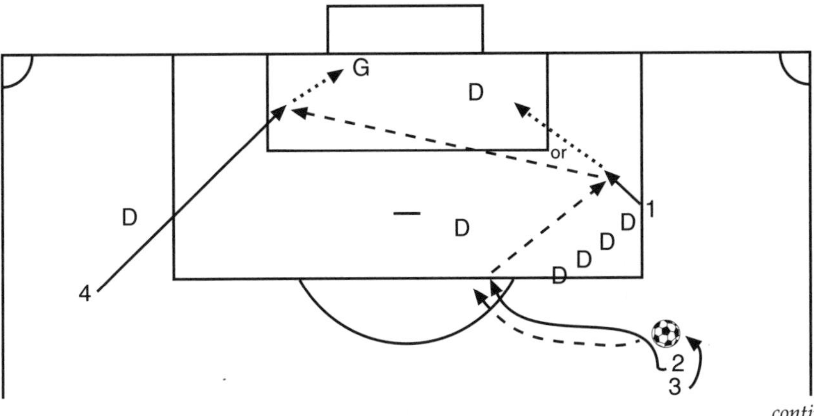

continued

Liner Combo *(continued)*

Variation 2

2 runs over the ball and past the far-post side of the defensive wall. 3 makes a chip pass over the wall to 1, who runs behind the wall as soon as the ball is passed. The intent of 2's run is to draw a defender from behind the wall, creating space for 1. 1 shoots on goal or passes to 4, who has made a timed run to the far post to be in position for a possible pass and first-time shot on goal.

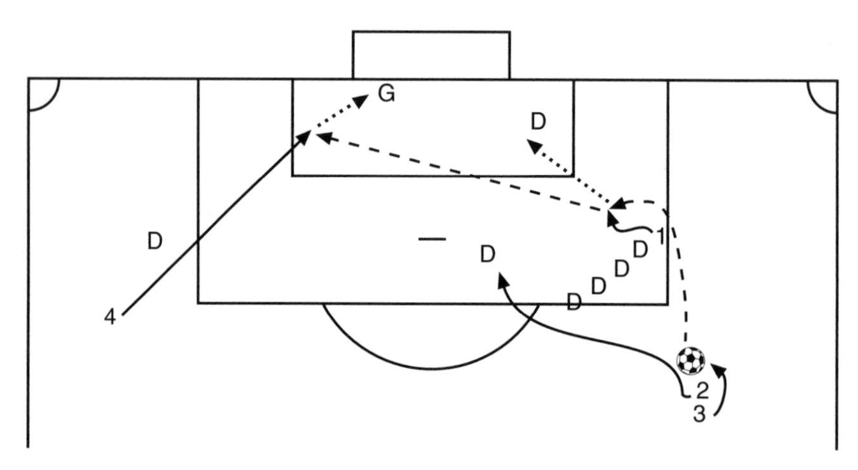

Defensive Tips

Defenders must quickly set up a three- to four-player wall with the tallest player at the near-post end. The goalkeeper covers the far post and must be able to see the ball. A defender not in the wall covers 2 to keep the attacker from being unmarked in a key central area, and another defender prevents 4 from getting goal-side.

Offensive Tips

2 or 3 may take a direct shot on goal if the wall is not set quickly or effectively and there is open space at either post. 4 makes an aggressive run to get goal-side and be first to the ball.

Contributor: William J. Viger, Boys' Coach, North Cobb High School, Kennesaw, Georgia

Off the Wall

Formation

The ball is placed five yards outside the left side of the 18-yard line. Attackers 1 and 4 are in position to take the free kick. Attacker 2 is standing at the near-post end of the defensive wall. Attacker 3, as a decoy, stands 10 yards in front and to the left of 4. Attackers 5 and 6 are at the right side of the penalty area.

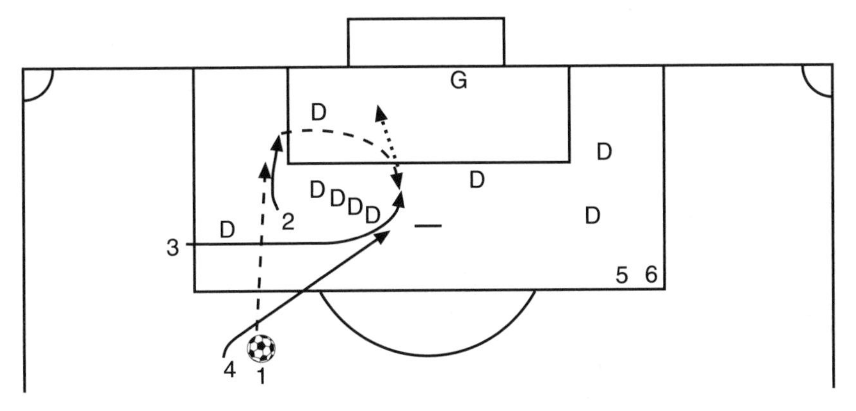

Procedure

3 sprints toward the penalty line. 4 runs over the ball toward the penalty line. If the defender moves with 3, 1 plays the ball on the ground to the side of 2. 2, whose back is to the wall to shield against those players, follows the ball as it runs on and makes a cross to the penalty line for either 3 or 4 to shoot on goal.

Variation 1

3 sprints toward the penalty line. 4 runs over the ball toward the penalty line. If the defender moves with 3, 1 plays the ball on the ground to the side of 2. 2 dribbles the ball toward the goal line and crosses to the far post to 5 and 6, who have run toward the goal area. Whoever gets the ball shoots on goal.

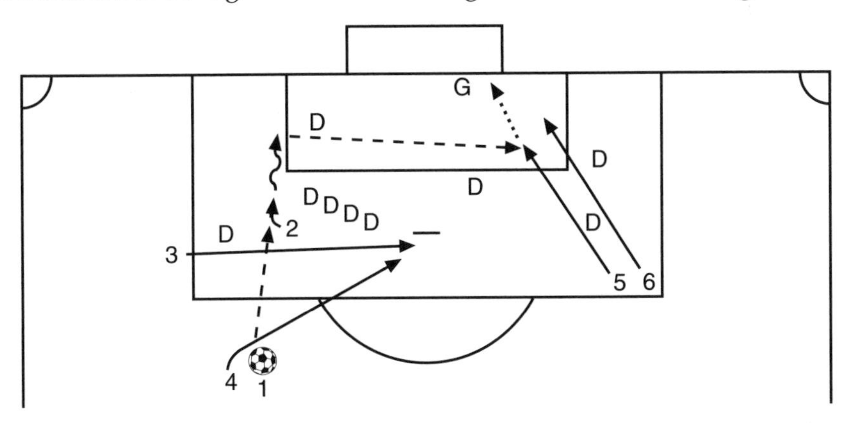

continued

Off the Wall *(continued)*

Variation 2

3 sprints toward the penalty line. 4 runs over the ball toward the penalty line. If the defender does not follow 3, 1 plays the ball to the far post to 5 and 6, who have run toward the goal area. Whoever gets the ball shoots on goal. 2 follows the pass to the goal to be in position for a possible rebound.

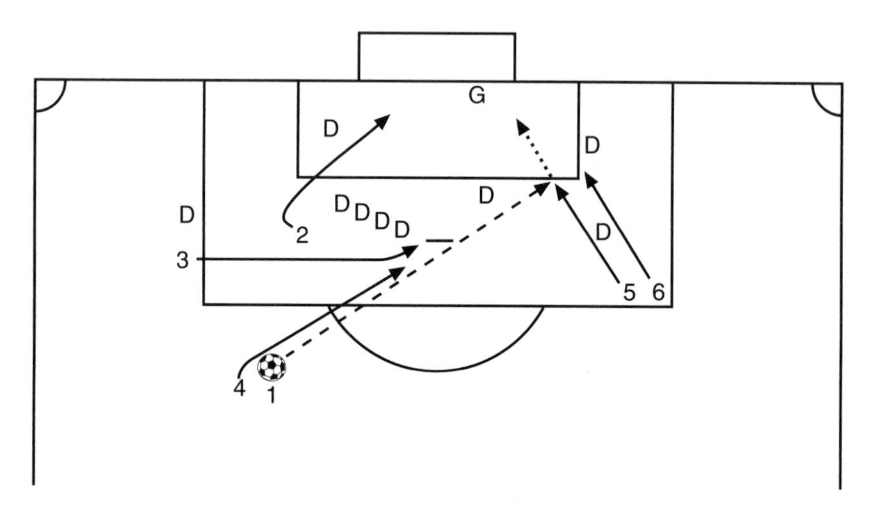

Defensive Tips

Defenders quickly set a four- to five-player wall with the tallest player at the near-post end. The goalkeeper covers the far post and must be able to see the ball. Defenders not in the wall follow the runs of 2, 3, and 4 to keep them from being unmarked in the central scoring area. Players defending against 5 and 6 must keep them from getting goal-side.

Offensive Tips

1 or 4 can take a direct shot on goal if the wall is not set quickly or effectively and if space is open at either post. 5 and 6 make aggressive runs to get goal-side and be first to the ball.

Contributor: David W. Wright, Men's Coach, Gettysburg College, Gettysburg, Pennsylvania

Open Player on End of Wall

Formation

The ball is placed 10 yards outside the right side of the 18-yard line. Attackers 2 and 3 are in position to take the free kick. Attacker 1 is at the near-post end of the defensive wall. Attackers 4 and 5 stand on the left side of the penalty area.

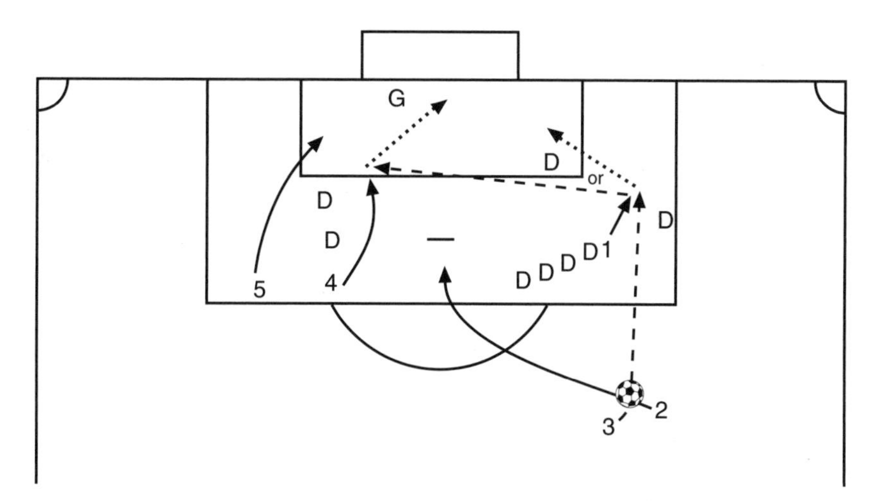

Procedure

If 1 is free, the play is on. 2 runs over the ball toward the penalty line to draw attention. 3 sends a crisp, rolling ball ahead of 1. 1 must turn and, within two or three steps, strike the ball low on goal to the near post or pass it in the air to the far post for 4 and 5, who are crashing to the far-post area. Whoever gets the ball shoots on goal.

continued

Open Player on End of Wall *(continued)*

Variation

If 1 is marked, 3 rolls the ball to 2, who shoots on goal or makes a chip pass to the far post for 4 or 5 to make a head shot on goal.

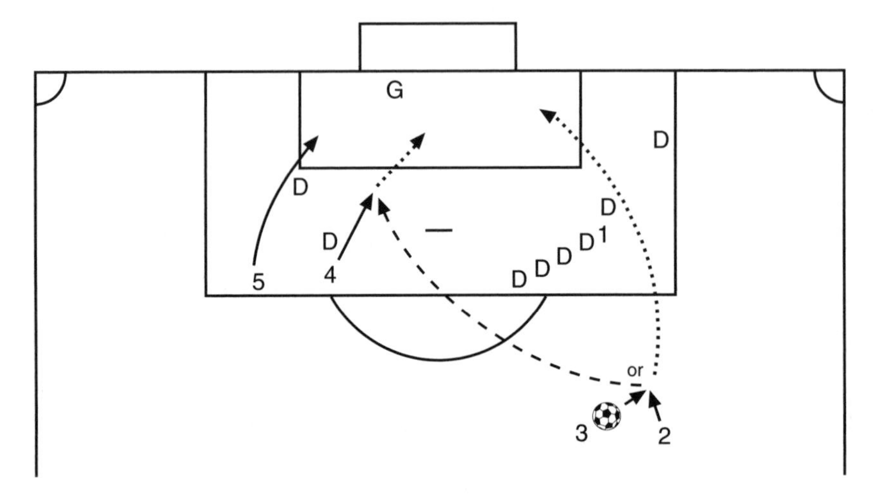

Defensive Tips

Defenders quickly set a three- to four-player wall with the tallest player at the near-post end. The goalkeeper covers the far post and must be able to see the ball. A player not in the wall covers 2's run, and other defenders keep 4 and 5 from getting goal-side.

Offensive Tips

If the wall is not set quickly or effectively, 2 can take a direct shot to the far post or 3 can take a direct shot to the near post. 4 and 5 make aggressive runs to get goal-side and be first to the ball.

Contributor: Loren E. Kline, Former Men's Coach, University of Delaware, Newark, Delaware

Options

Formation

The ball is placed 5 to 10 yards outside the right side of the 18-yard line. Attackers 1 and 2 are in position to take the free kick. Attacker 3 is five yards to the left of the ball. Attacker 4 is directly behind 3. Attackers 5 and 6 stand outside the left side of the penalty area.

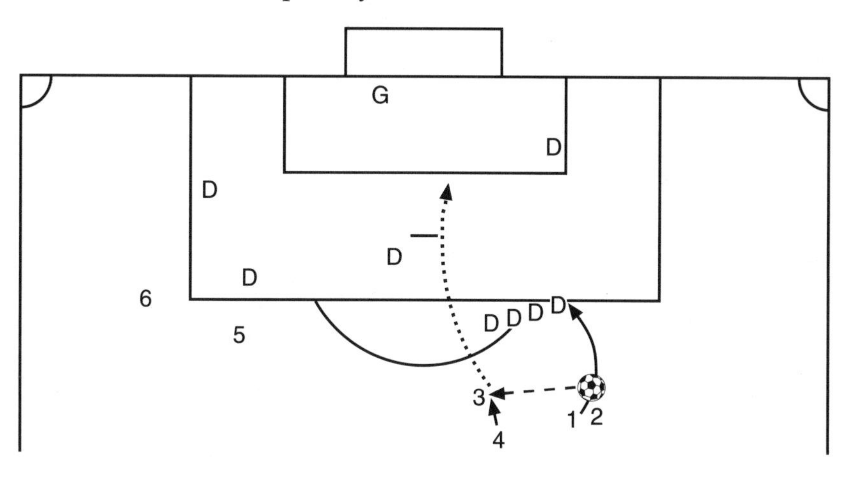

Procedure

1 runs over the ball toward the near-post end of the defensive wall. 2 passes square to 3, who stops the ball for 4, who shoots directly on goal.

Variation 1

1 runs over the ball and past the near-post end of the defensive wall. 2 plays the ball wide to 1. 1 shoots on goal or passes to 5 and 6, who have run toward the far post. Whoever gets the ball shoots on goal.

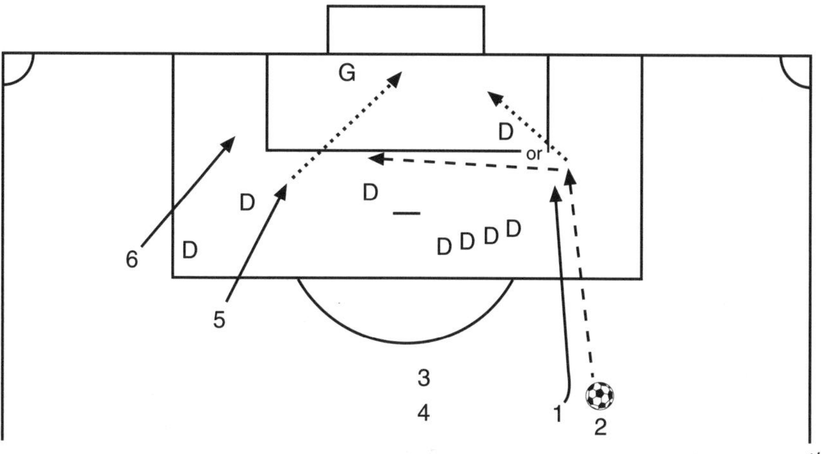

continued

Variation 2

1 runs over the ball toward the near-post end of the defensive wall. 2 passes to 5 or 6, who have made wide runs toward the far post. Whoever gets the ball shoots on goal.

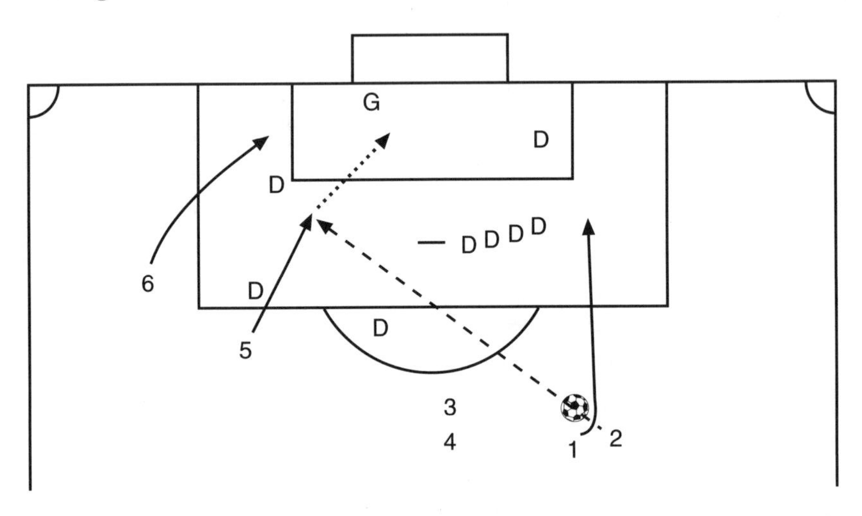

Defensive Tips

Defenders quickly set a three- to four-player wall with the tallest player at the near-post end. The goalkeeper covers the far post and must be able to see the ball. A player not in the wall marks 1. Those defending against 5 and 6 must try to prevent them from getting goal-side. The wall defenders break as soon as the first pass is made and move to pressure the player with the ball and nearby attackers.

Offensive Tips

1 or 2 may take a direct shot on goal if either player sees open space at the near post. 2 must be able to make crisp, accurate passes. 5 and 6 make aggressive runs to get goal-side and be first to the ball.

Contributor: Jim Felix, Boys' Coach, Buckingham, Browne and Nichols School, Cambridge, Massachusetts

Penmen Special

Formation The ball is placed 10 yards outside the right side of the 18-yard line. Attacker 1 is in position to take the free kick. Attackers 2 and 3 are to the left side and slightly in front of the defensive wall. Attacker 4 is 10 yards to the left of the far-post end of the defensive wall.

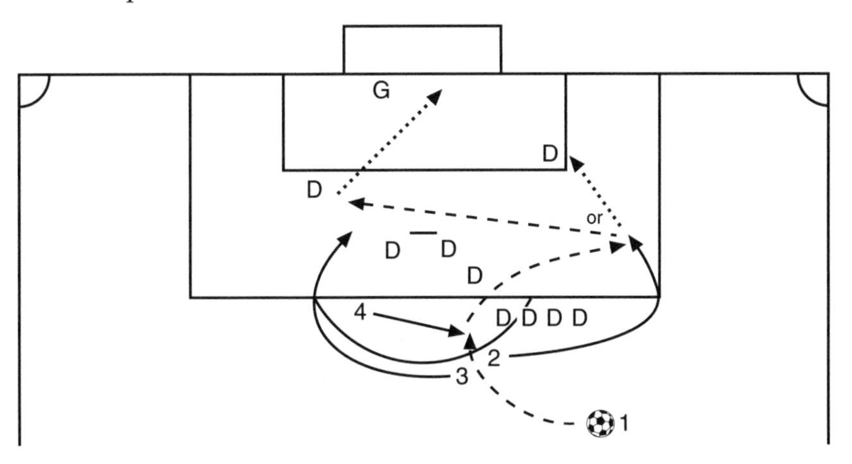

Procedure 2 walks toward the near-post end of the defensive wall. As 2 reaches the end of the wall, 3 makes a curling run toward the far post. 4 checks toward 1. 1 plays the ball to 4. 4 makes a one-touch pass to 2, who began to run behind the wall as soon as the first pass was made. 2 shoots on goal or passes to 3, who shoots on goal.

Variation 1 2 walks toward the near-post end of the defensive wall. As 2 reaches the end of the wall, 3 makes a curling run toward the far post. 4 checks toward 1. 1 makes a chip pass over the wall to 2, who shoots on goal or passes toward the far post to 3, who shoots on goal.

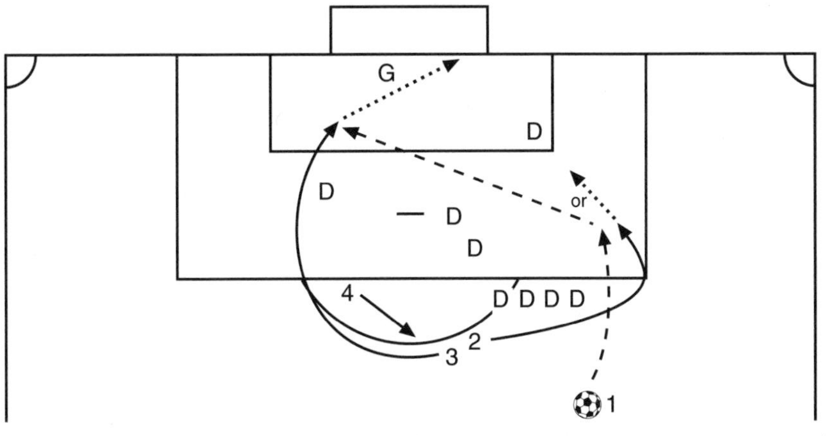

continued

Variation 2

2 walks toward the near-post end of the defensive wall. As 2 reaches the end of the wall, 3 makes a curling run toward the far post. 4 checks toward 1. 1 makes a chip pass over the wall to the far post to 3. 3 takes a first-time shot on goal or passes to 2 and 4, who have run toward the goal area to be in position for a possible pass and shot on goal.

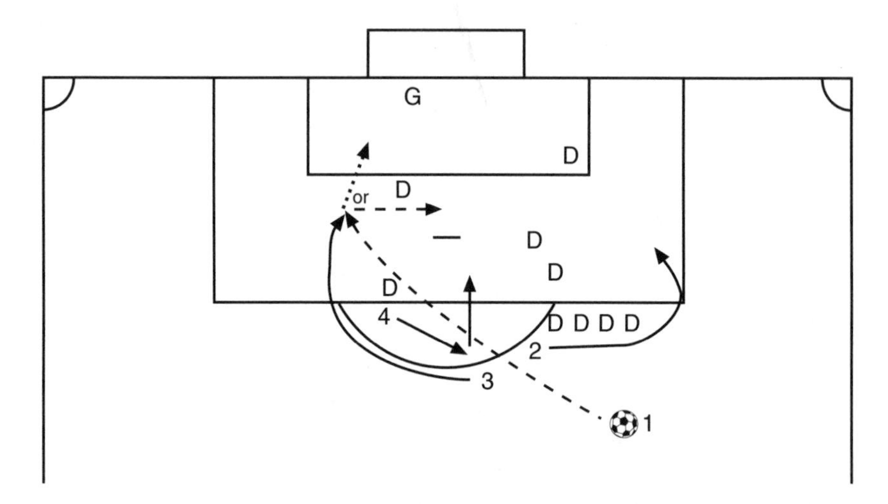

Defensive Tips

Defenders quickly set a three- to four-player wall with the tallest player at the near-post end. The goalkeeper covers the far post and must be able to see the ball. Defenders not in the wall must not leave attackers making decoy runs unmarked in the central scoring area. A defender must prevent 3 from getting goal-side.

Offensive Tips

Since this play requires excellent ball handling and well-timed decoy runs, it should be used only by advanced teams.

Contributor: John T. Rootes, Men's Coach, New Hampshire College, Manchester, New Hampshire

Player Isolation

Formation

The ball is placed at midfield on the right side of the field. Attacker 1 is in position to take the free kick. Attacker 4 is a few yards behind and to the left of 1. Attacker 2 is at the top of the center circle in the attacking half of the field. Most of the remaining attackers are spread throughout the attacking half of the field with attacker 3, the target player, in the left side of the penalty area.

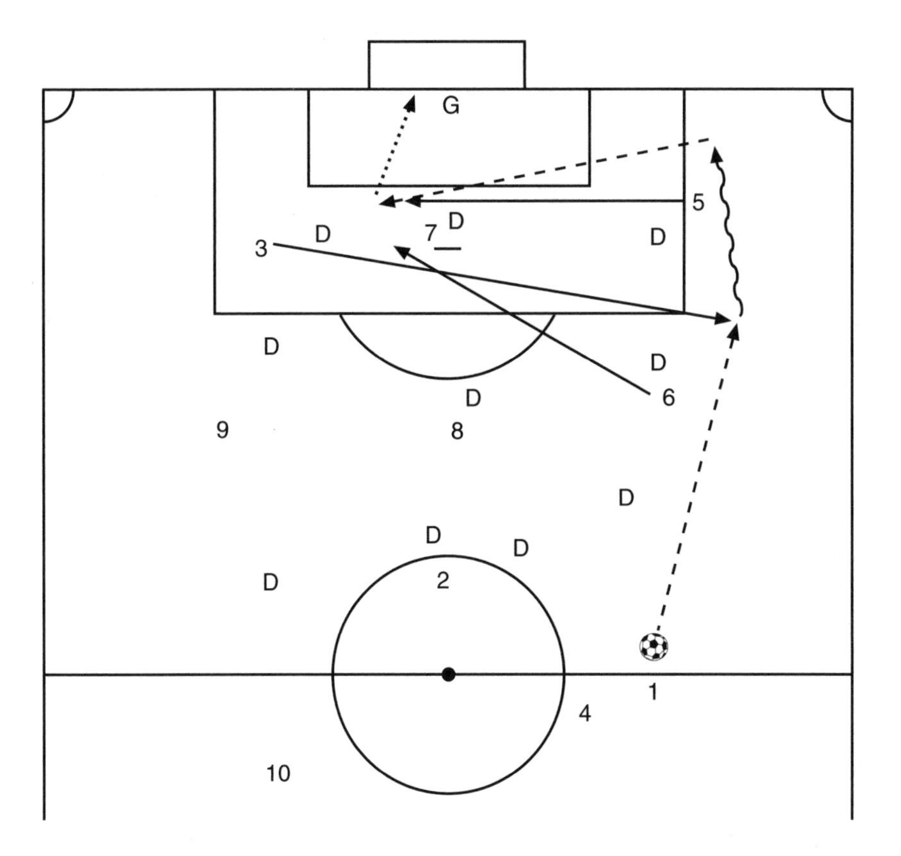

Procedure

5 and 6 attempt to take their defenders out of the passing lane of 1 by running toward 3. 3 runs toward the area vacated by 5 and 6 and receives a pass from 1. 3 carries the ball down the wing and crosses it to 5 or 6 on the opposite side of the field. The first player to get the ball takes a first-time shot on goal.

continued

Player Isolation *(continued)*

Variation 1

5 and 6 take their defenders out of the passing lane of 1 by running toward 3. 3 runs toward the area vacated by 5 and 6. 2 moves forward to the right, receives a pass from 1, and carries the ball down the wing to cross to 5, 6, or 7. The first player to get the ball takes a first-time shot on goal.

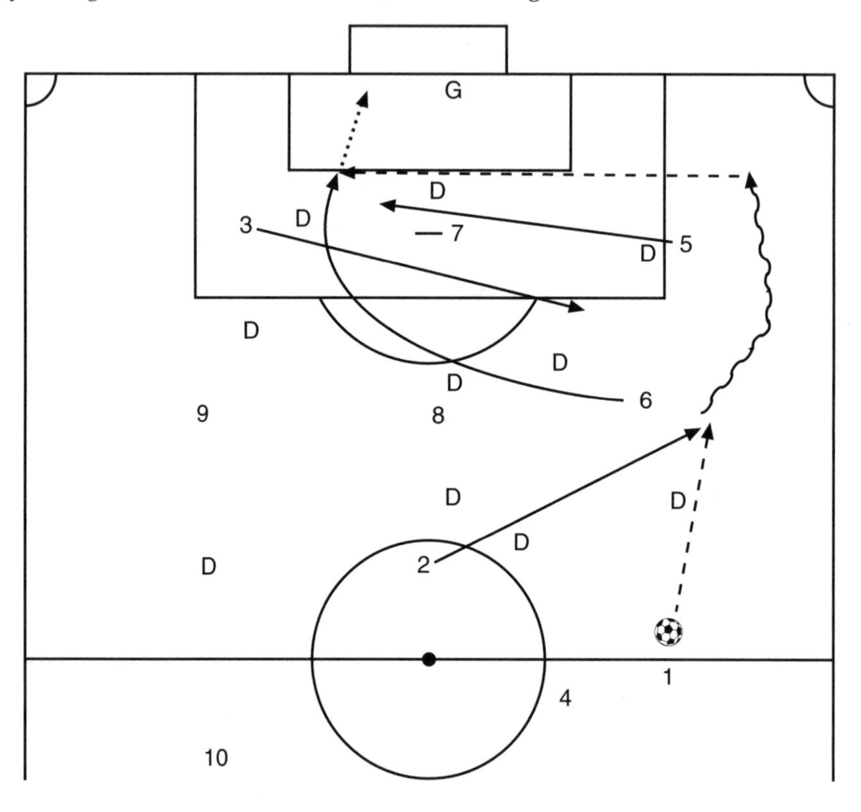

Variation 2

5 and 6 take their defenders out of the passing lane of 1 by running toward 3. 3 runs toward the area vacated by 5 and 6. 1 fakes a pass and runs over the ball. 4 moves to the ball and touches it down the line to 1, who crosses it to 5, 6, or 7. The first player to get the ball takes a first-time shot on goal.

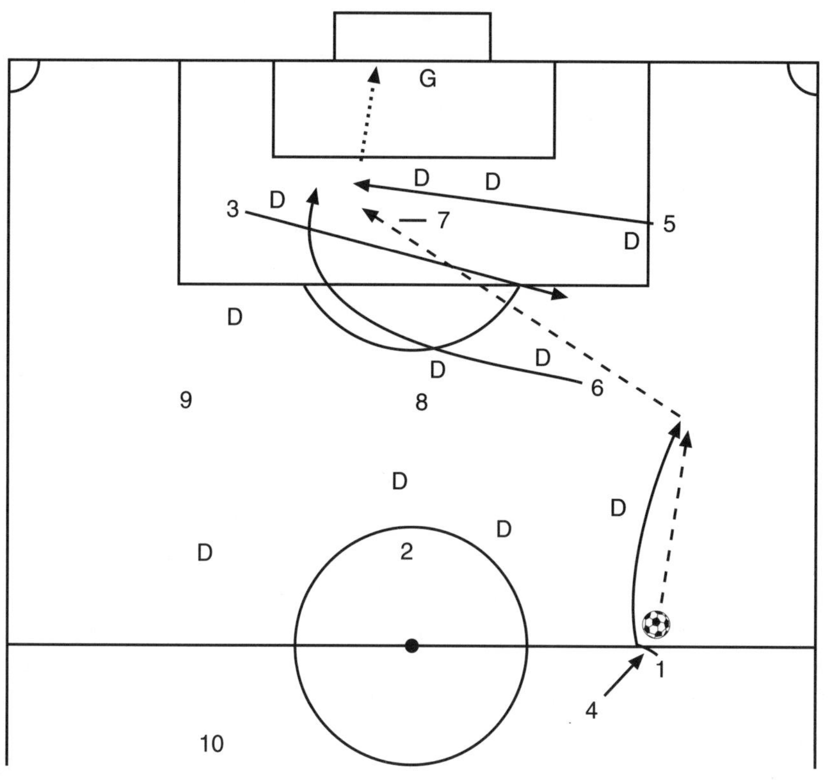

Defensive Tips

Players move quickly to cover attackers one on one near the ball. Other defenders must be alert to prevent attackers from getting goal-side. A defender must cover 3's runs.

Offensive Tips

Attackers must play the ball quickly to take advantage of any defensive confusion. The aim is to get the ball behind the defense quickly. Whenever a numerical advantage occurs, those players must exploit the situation immediately and go for goal. 3 can turn and move to the goal for a shot if not marked when making a decoy run. 5 and 6 must make their runs aggressively and try to be first to any ball passed to them. 7 stays alert for a rebound or weak clear.

Contributor: Larry M. Gross, Former Women's Coach, North Carolina State University, Raleigh, North Carolina

Pull

Formation

The ball is placed 10 yards outside the right side of the 18-yard line and 25 yards from the goal line. Attackers 2 and 3 are in position to take the free kick. Attacker 1 stands at the far-post end of the defensive wall. Attackers 4, 5, 6, and 7 stand in a line on the left side of the 18-yard line.

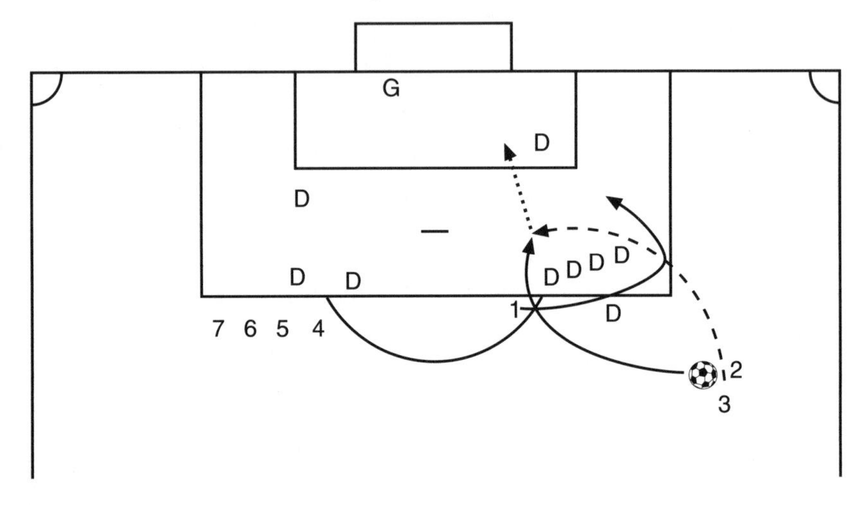

Procedure

On a prearranged signal, 1 sprints around the front of the defensive wall and then toward the near post. At the same time 2 sprints over the ball and past the far-post end of the wall. 3 makes a chip pass over the wall to either 1 or 2, who shoots on goal. 4, 5, 6, and 7 create space for 1 and 2 by maintaining their positions and keeping their defenders' attention on them.

Defensive Tips

Defenders quickly set a three- to four-player wall with the tallest player at the near-post end. The goalkeeper covers the far post and must be able to see the ball. Players not in the wall must cover the runs of 1 and 2 to prevent them from being unmarked.

Offensive Tips

If the wall is not set quickly or effectively, 2 or 3 can take a direct shot to either post. 4, 5, 6, and 7 stay alert for weak clears.

Contributor: Bob Winch, Men's Coach, University of Central Florida, Orlando, Florida

Run Over and Shoot

Formation

The ball is placed five yards outside the middle of the 18-yard line. Attackers 1, 2, and 3 are in position to take the free kick. Attackers 4 and 5 stand in front of the defensive wall facing the ball.

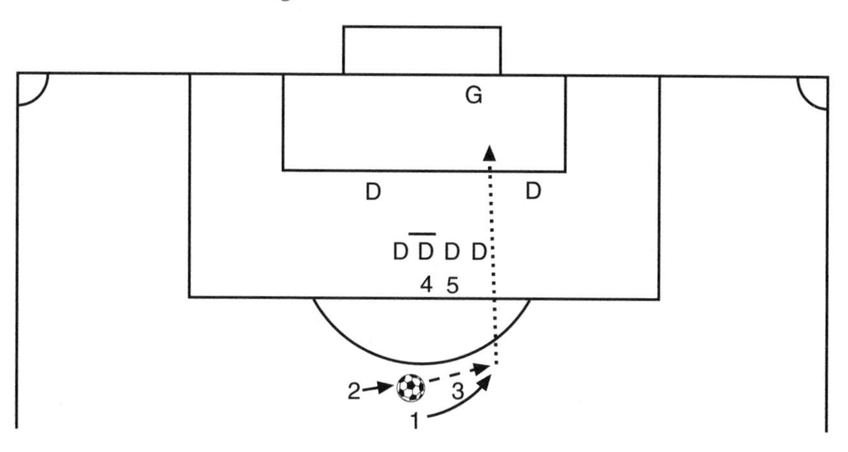

Procedure

2 rolls the ball between 3's legs while 1 moves forward and to the right to take a shot on goal around the wall. The shot can be taken toward either post depending on the setup of the defensive wall and the goalkeeper's position. 4 and 5 maintain their positions to obstruct the defenders' view.

Variation 1

1 runs over the ball. 3 runs forward and to the right. 2 passes to 3, who shoots on goal. 4 and 5 curl off opposite ends of the defensive wall before the shot and sprint to the goal to be in position for a possible rebound.

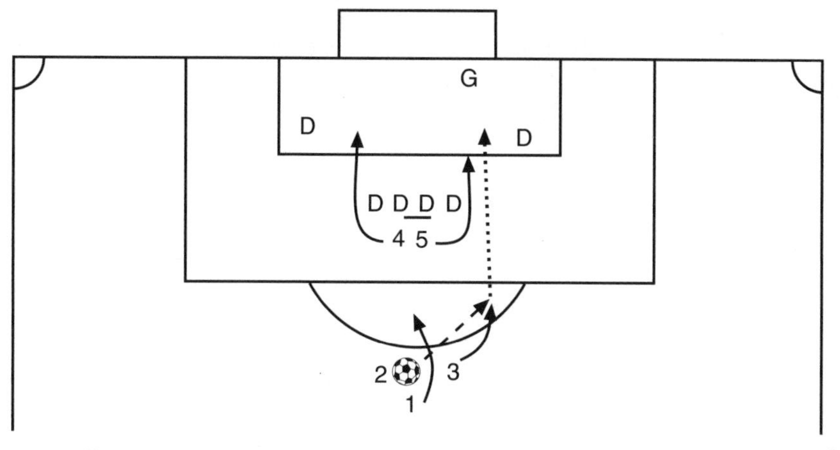

continued

Run Over and Shoot *(continued)*

Variation 2

4 and 5 curl around opposite ends of the defensive wall. 1 chips the ball over the wall to 4 or 5. Whoever gets the ball shoots on goal, and the other player follows up for a possible rebound.

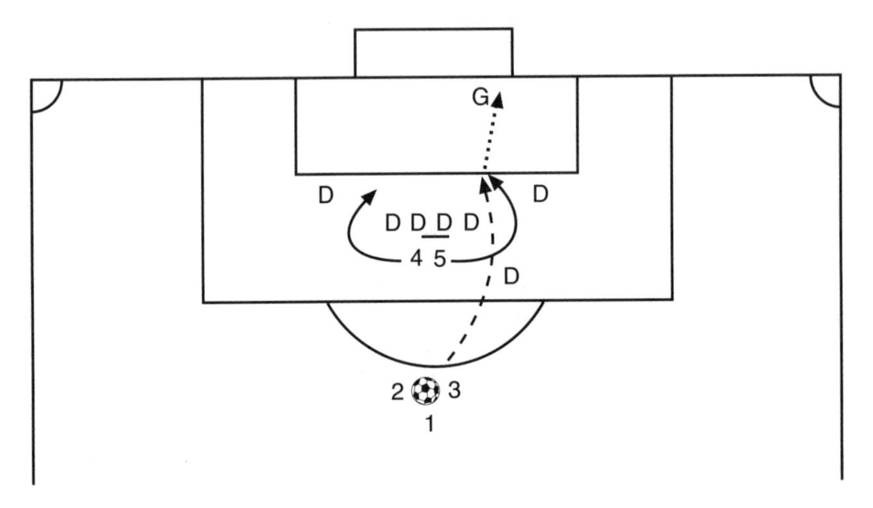

Defensive Tips

Defenders quickly set a four- to five-player wall with the tallest player at the near-post end. The goalkeeper covers the far post and must be able to see the ball. The wall players must not duck or turn on a blast shot. They break from the wall as soon as the first pass is made and move quickly to pressure the player with the ball and nearby players. Defenders not in the wall cover 4 and 5 so they are not left unmarked in the central scoring area.

Offensive Tips

On a direct free kick, 1, 2, or 3 may take a direct shot on goal if the wall is not set quickly or space is open at either corner.

Contributor: Robert G. Reasso, Men's Coach, Rutgers University, Piscataway, New Jersey

Shoot Through Wall

Formation

The ball is placed 10 yards outside the left side of the 18-yard line. Attacker 1 is in position to take the free kick. Attacker 2 is a yard to the right of the ball. Attacker 3 is 10 yards to the right of the ball. Attackers 4 and 5 are to the right and slightly in front of the far-post end of the defensive wall. Attackers 6 and 7 are about 10 yards to the right and left, respectively, of the defensive wall.

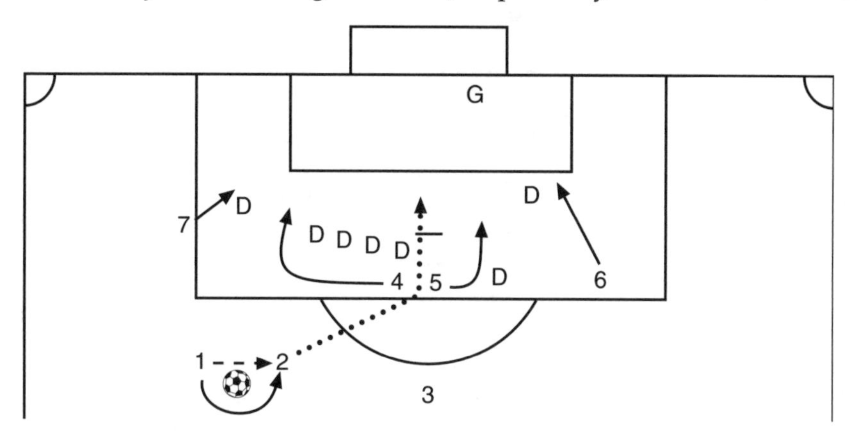

Procedure

1 taps the ball to 2. 2 controls the ball with a sole-of-the-foot trap. 1 follows up the pass and shoots on goal through the offensive wall set up by 4 and 5. 4, 5, 6, and 7 follow up the shot on goal to be in position for a possible rebound. 1, 2, and 3 maintain their positions to be ready for a possible long rebound.

Variation 1

1 makes a chip pass to 6, who sprints toward the far post and shoots on goal. 4, 5, and 7 follow up the shot to be in position for a possible rebound.

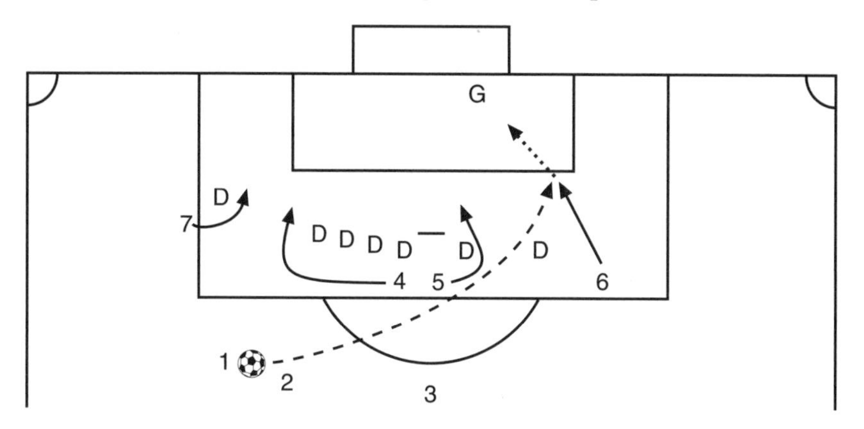

continued

Variation 2

1 passes to either 3 or 7, who sprints toward the goal area and shoots on goal. 4, 5, and 6 follow up the shot to be in position for a possible rebound.

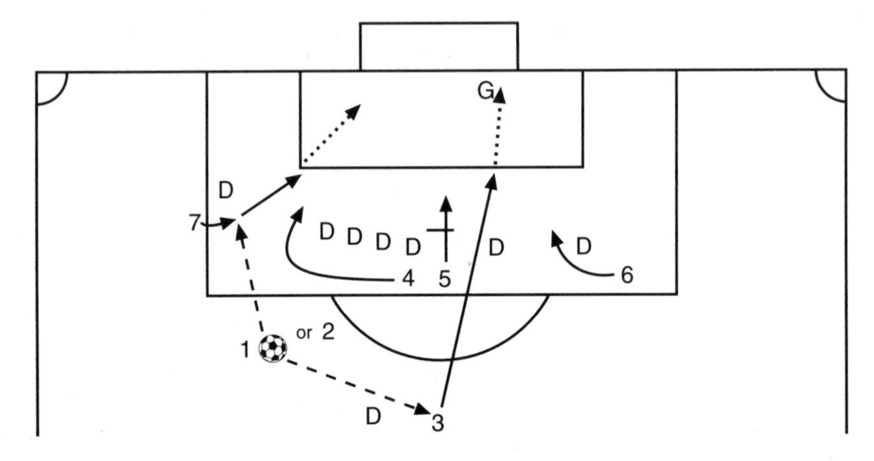

Defensive Tips

Defenders quickly set a three- to four-player wall with the tallest player at the near-post end. Defenders not in the wall cover 4 and 5 so they are not left unmarked in the central scoring area. The wall players break as soon as the first pass is made and challenge the player with the ball and nearby players. Those defending against 6 and 7 prevent them from getting goal-side.

Offensive Tips

1 can take a swerving shot on goal if it is a direct free kick and space is open at either post. 4, 5, 6, and 7 must try to get goal-side and be first to the ball.

Contributor: Keith D. Tabatznik, Men's Coach, Georgetown University, Washington, D.C.

Spin and Shoot

Formation The ball is placed just outside the right side of the penalty-area restraining arc. Attacker 1 is in position to take the free kick. Attacker 3 is five yards to the left of 1. Attacker 2 is a few yards behind and to the left of 1.

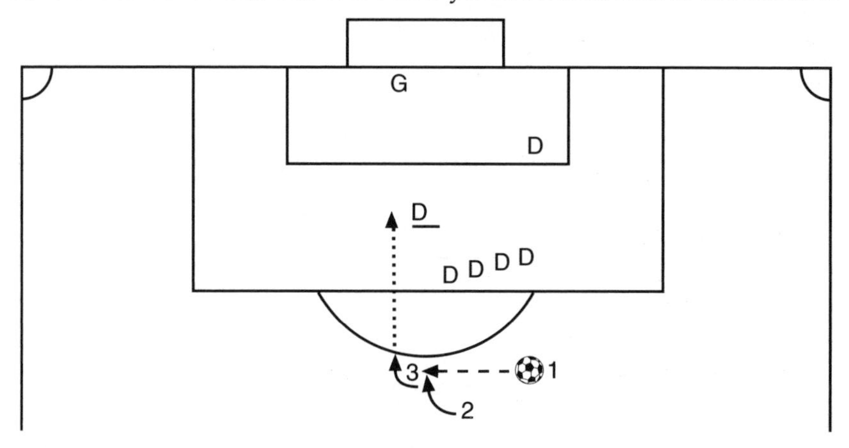

Procedure 1 passes to 3, who stops the ball with a sole-of-the-foot trap. 2 sprints toward the ball as if to take a shot on goal. 3 holds the ball to commit the defense to block the shot. 3 then spins outside with the ball and takes a left-footed shot on goal.

Variation 1 backheels the ball to 2, who runs behind 1 and takes a right-footed shot on goal around the near-post end of the defensive wall.

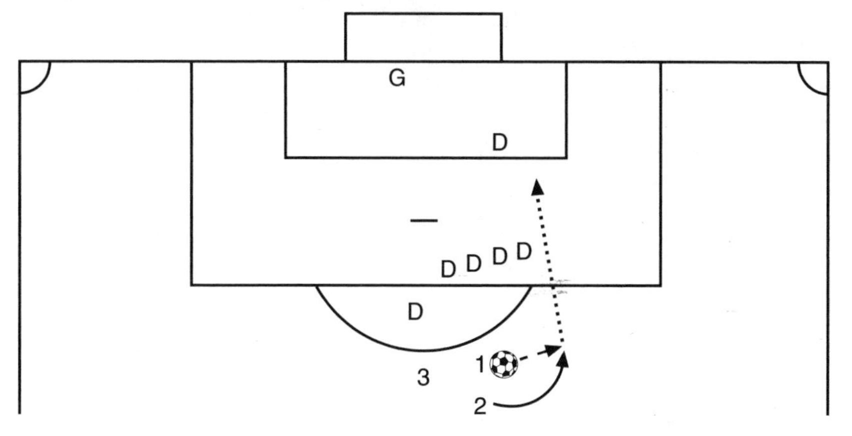

Defensive Tips Defenders quickly set a four- to five-player wall with the tallest player at the near-post end. The goalkeeper covers the far post and must be able to see the ball. Players in the wall break as soon as the first pass is made and move to pressure the player with the ball and nearby attackers.

Offensive Tips On a direct free kick play, 1 can shoot on goal if space is open at either post.

Contributor: Gary R. Parsons, Men's Coach, Oakland University, Rochester, Michigan

Straight Shooter

Formation

The ball is placed 10 yards outside the right side of the 18-yard line. Attackers 1, 2, and 3 are in position to take the free kick. Attackers 4 and 5 stand on opposite ends of the defensive wall. Attackers 6 and 7 stand just outside the left side of the 18-yard line.

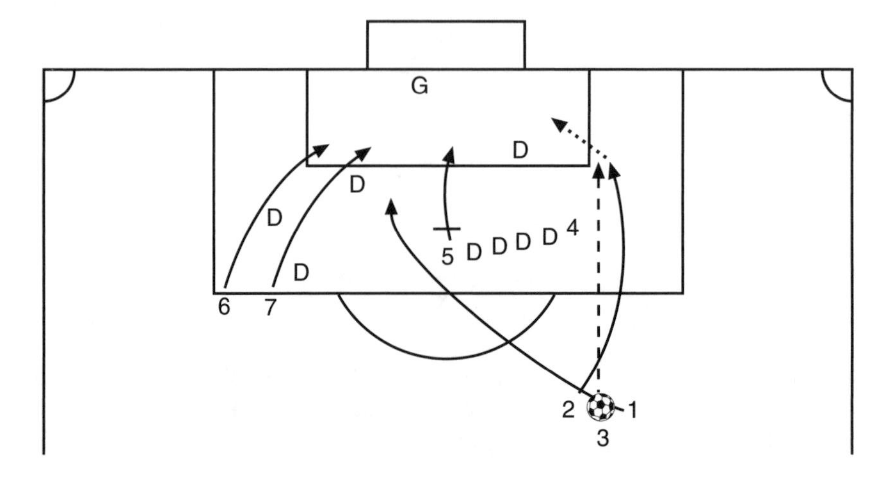

Procedure

1 runs over the ball and around the far-post end of the defensive wall. 2 runs over the ball and around 4 at the near-post end of the defensive wall. 3 plays the ball firmly on the ground to 2, timing the pass so that the ball and 2 arrive at the same time in the area behind and to the right of the near-post end of the defensive wall. 2 takes a first-time shot on goal. 4 holds a firm position to screen the end defensive player until the pass is made. 5, 6, and 7, who moved into the goal area immediately after the pass, follow up the shot on goal to be in position for a possible rebound.

Variation

1 runs over the ball and around the far-post end of the defensive wall. 2 runs over the ball and around 4 at the near-post end of the defensive wall. 3 plays the ball firmly on the ground to 2, timing the pass so that the ball and 2 arrive at the same time in the area behind and to the right of the near-post end of the defensive wall. If a reasonable shot is not possible, 2 plays the ball across the goal mouth toward 5, 6, and 7, who moved into the goal area immediately after the pass. Whoever gets the ball shoots on goal.

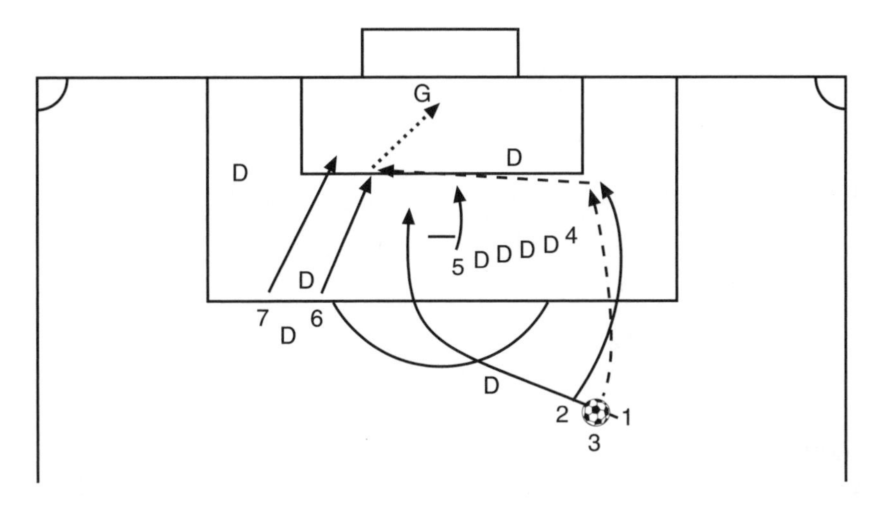

Defensive Tips

Defenders quickly set a three- to four-player wall with the tallest player at the near-post end. The goalkeeper covers the far post and must be able to see the ball. Players not in the wall cover 1, 2, and 5 so they are not left unmarked in the central scoring area. Defenders must keep 6 and 7 from getting goal-side.

Offensive Tips

On a direct free kick, 3 can take a swerving shot over or around 4, who ducks or turns as the shot is taken. Attackers make aggressive runs to get goal-side and be first to the ball. All attackers stay alert for rebounds or weak clears.

Contributor: Joseph A. Amorim, Men's Coach, Haverford College, Haverford, Pennsylvania

Three-Player Combo

Formation

The ball is placed 15 yards outside the left side of the 18-yard line. Attackers 4 and 5 are in position to take the free kick. Attackers 3, 2, 1, and 6 line up to the right of the ball from left to right respectively, in staggered positions. 7 stands to the left of the ball near the sideline.

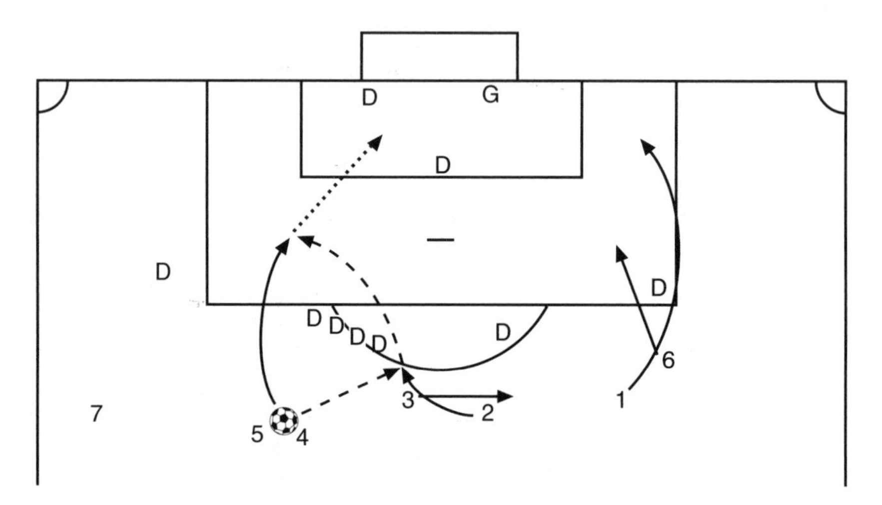

Procedure

4 runs over the ball toward the near-post end of the defensive wall. 2 and 3 switch positions. 6 slowly runs toward the middle of the penalty area, while 1 loops around 6 toward the far post. 5 passes to 2, who makes a first-time pass behind the defensive wall to 4, who has run past the near-post end of the wall to meet the ball. 4 takes a shot on goal. 1 and 6 stay alert for a possible rebound.

Variation

4 runs over the ball toward the near-post end of the defensive wall. 2 and 3 switch positions. 6 slowly runs toward the middle of the penalty area, while 1 loops around 6 toward the far post. 5 passes to 2, who makes a first-time pass behind the defensive wall to 4, who has run past the near-post end of the wall to meet the pass. 4 passes to 1 at the far post. 1 shoots on goal. 6 stays alert for a possible rebound.

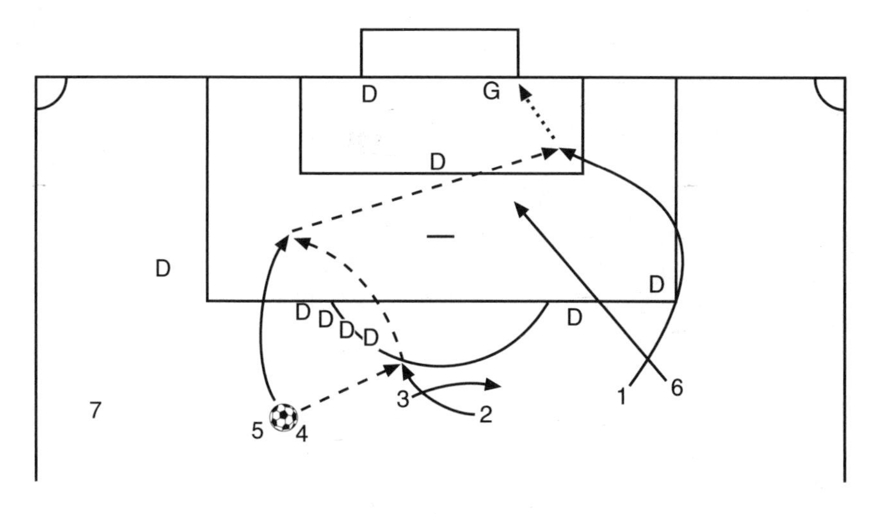

Defensive Tips

Defenders quickly set a three- to four-player wall with the tallest player at the near-post end. The goalkeeper covers the far post and must be able to see the ball. Defenders not in the wall cover attackers making runs to prevent them from getting goal-side or being open in the central scoring area. The wall defenders break from the wall as soon as the first pass is made and move to challenge the player with the ball and any open attackers.

Offensive Tips

On a direct kick, 4 or 5 may take a shot on goal if the wall is not set quickly and space is open at either post. This play requires effective runs and precision passes, and it should not be attempted by novice teams.

Contributor: Bob A. Dikranian, Former Men's Coach, Southern Connecticut State University, New Haven, Connecticut

Through the Gap

Formation

The ball is placed 10 yards outside the left side of the 18-yard line. Attackers 1 and 3 are in position to take the free kick. Attacker 2 stands at the far-post end of the defensive wall. Attackers 4 and 5 stand just outside the right side of the penalty area.

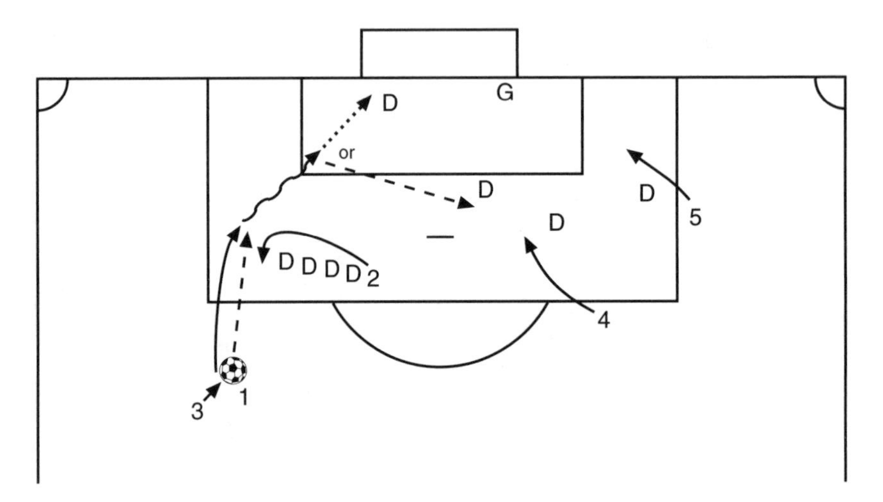

Procedure

1 runs over the ball and stops just outside the near-post end of the defensive wall. Simultaneously, 2 moves behind the wall to a position off the shoulder of the defender at the near-post end. 3 then passes the ball through the gap created by 1 and 2. 1 moves with the ball and either shoots on goal or passes to 4 or 5, who are sprinting toward the goal.

Defensive Tips

Defenders quickly set a three- to four-player wall with the tallest player at the near-post end. The goalkeeper covers the far post and must be able to see the ball. Defenders not in the wall cover 1, 2, 4, and 5 to prevent them from getting goal-side or being unmarked in the central scoring area.

Offensive Tips

1 or 3 can take a direct shot on goal. 4 and 5 make aggressive runs to get goal-side.

Contributor: Sigi Schmid, Men's Coach, University of California, Los Angeles, Los Angeles, California

Through the Legs

Formation

The ball is placed five yards outside the right side of the 18-yard line. Attackers 1, 2, and 3 are in position to take the free kick, with 2 to the right of 1, and 3 a few yards farther away from goal and behind 2. 4 stands about 10 yards to the left of and a little behind 1.

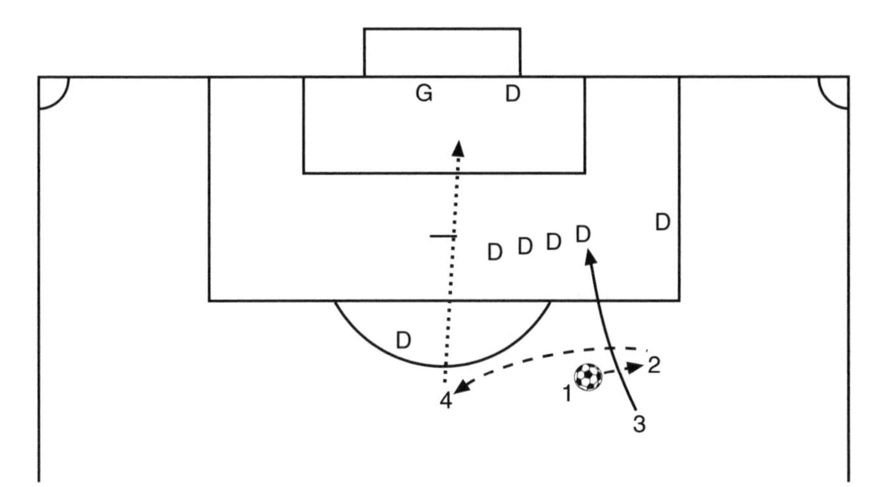

Procedure

1 rolls the ball to 2, who stops it. 3 runs over the ball toward the defensive wall. 2 passes the ball through the legs of 1 to 4, who takes a first-time shot on goal.

Defensive Tips

Defenders quickly set a three- to four-player wall with the tallest player at the near-post end. The goalkeeper covers the far post and must be able to see the ball. Players in the wall move to challenge the player with the ball and any open attackers as soon as the first pass is made.

Offensive Tips

On a direct free kick, 1, 2, or 3 can take a shot on goal if space is open at either post.

Contributor: Andy Jennings, Athletic Director, Vassar College, Poughkeepsie, New York

Toxic

Formation

The ball is placed just inside the extreme right side of the 18-yard line. Attackers 1 and 2 are in position to take the free kick. Attacker 3 stands 10 yards to the left of the ball. Attacker 4 stands a few yards farther away from the goal and behind 3. Attacker 5 stands a few yards to the left of 4.

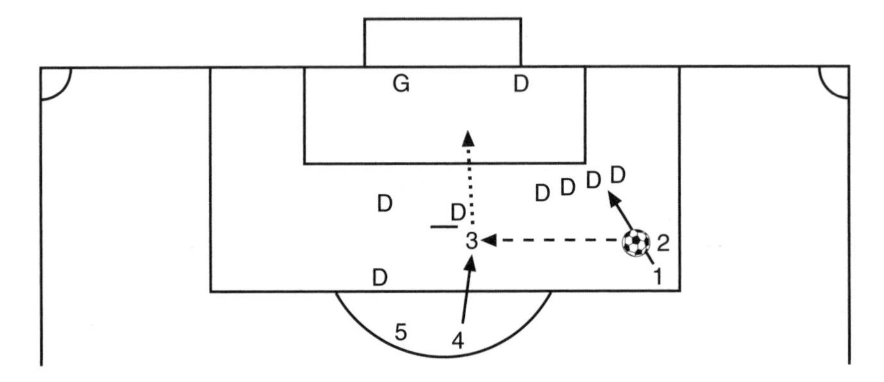

Procedure

1 runs over the ball toward the defensive wall. 2 immediately passes the ball to 3. 3 stops the ball with a sole-of-the-foot trap. 4 moves forward quickly and takes a shot on goal.

Variation

1 runs over the ball toward the defensive wall. 2 immediately passes the ball to 3. 3 lets the ball through to 5, while 4 serves as a decoy by running forward as the pass is made. 5 shoots on goal.

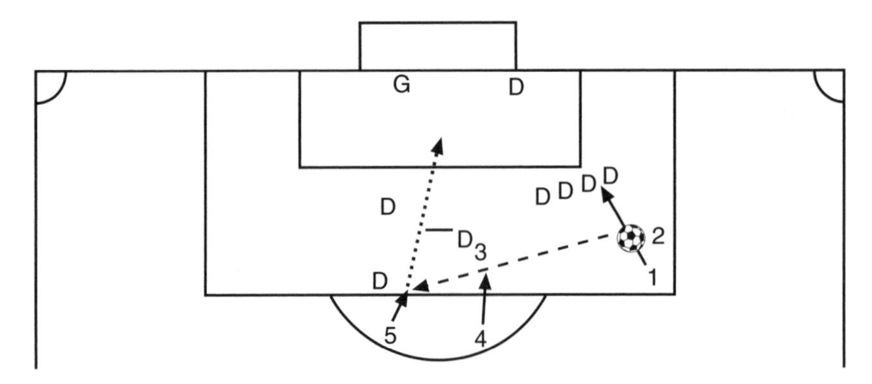

Defensive Tips

Defenders quickly set a four- to five-player wall with the tallest player at the near-post end. As the spot of the foul is within the penalty area, the coach may wish to have more players in the wall. Other defenders need to be alert to come back should the play bring more attackers into the area.

Offensive Tips

Although the indirect shot can be to either post, a near-post shot is preferable if the ball is passed quickly enough to beat the angle of the defensive wall and if the goalkeeper is covering the far post.

Contributor: Karen S. Stanely, Women's Coach, Santa Rosa Junior College, Santa Rosa, California

Triangular Series

Formation

The ball is placed five yards outside the left side of the 18-yard line. Attackers 1, 2, and 3 are in position to take the free kick in a triangle formation, each player two feet from the ball.

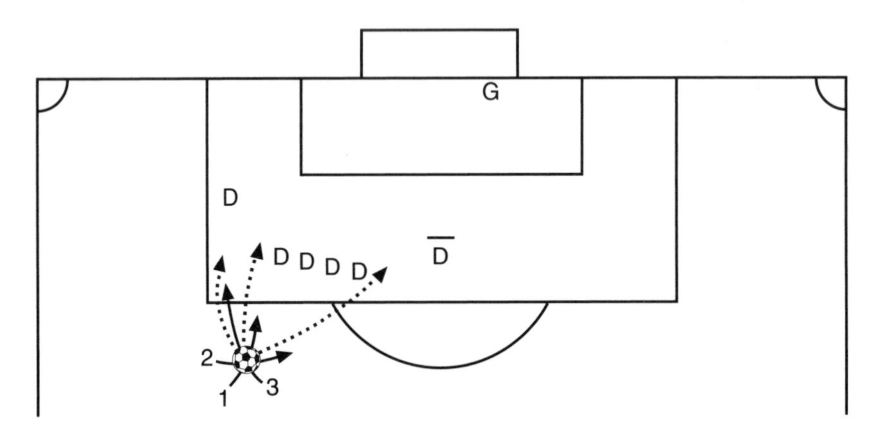

Procedure

There are numerous shooting options from the starting formation. 1 chooses which option to implement. 1, 2, or 3 approaches the ball as if to take a shot on goal. A player runs over the ball; a second may follow. Another player—or the last one left—takes a direct shot on goal.

Defensive Tips

Defenders quickly set a three- to four-player wall with the tallest player at the near-post end. The goalkeeper covers the far post and must be able to see the ball. Players in the wall must not duck or turn on the shot, and they break from the wall as soon as the pass is made to pressure the player with the ball and any open attackers.

Offensive Tips

If, on a direct free kick, the wall is not set quickly or effectively or there is open space at either post, 1 may take a shot on goal. For indirect kicks, one of the players running over the ball moves it no less than its circumference, and one of the other players follows with a shot on goal.

Contributor: John A. Reeves, Director of Physical Education and Intercollegiate Athletics, Columbia University, New York, New York

Ultra Challenge

Formation

The ball is placed 30 yards from the goal line on the left side of the field. Attacker 1 is in position to take the free kick. Attackers 2, 3, 4, and 5 are spread out on the right side of the field.

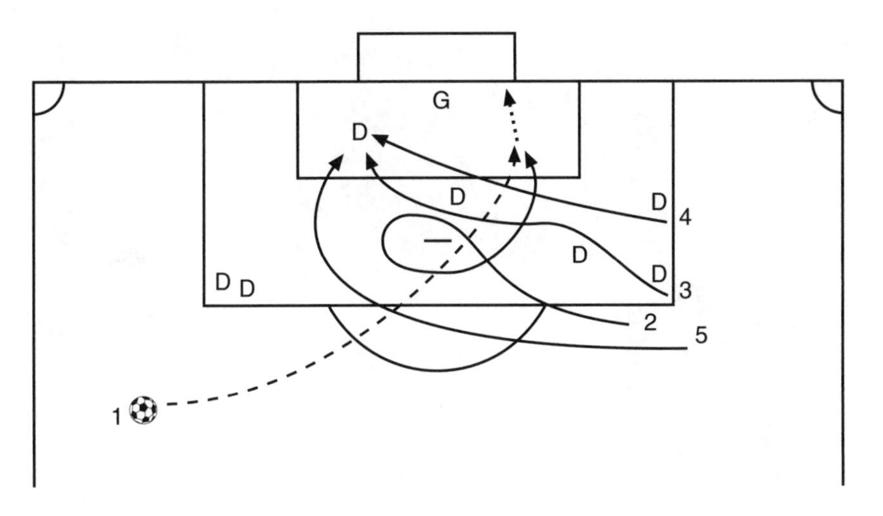

Procedure

2 is the key figure in this restart. As 1 prepares for the kick, 2 sprints toward the near post. 1 does not pass the ball. 2 circles back out and around toward the far post, moving slowly to avoid attracting attention. 3, 4, and 5 then sprint to the near post. 1 passes the ball to the far post to 2, who shoots on goal.

Defensive Tips

Defenders quickly set a two- to three-player wall. They must prevent 2, 3, 4, and 5 from getting goal-side or being unmarked in the central scoring area.

Offensive Tips

The attackers' runs must give a clear impression that the play will be to the near post. 2's final run must be aggressive to be first to the ball.

Contributors: I.M. Ibrahim, Former Men's Coach, Clemson University, Clemson, South Carolina and Bob Winch, Men's Coach, University of Central Florida, Orlando, Florida

Paul Martinez/PHOTOSPORT

PART II

THE CORNER KICK

In part I, we stressed the importance of preparing your team to act quickly and correctly in free-kick situations. In the corner-kick situation, you have an added advantage—your players are in the area immediately in front of the goal they're attacking. Should the opponents react slowly in setting up their defense, the same quick thinking and organization your team used in free kicks could result in a goal from a corner kick. However, because the defenders usually are in better positions than the attackers—and outnumber them in the goal area—a quick play is often counterproductive. Thus, it is better to take your time to set up a deliberate play.

In part II, we show you how to make the most of the corner-kick advantage. Chapter 3 covers corner-kick rules and prepares you to deal with the defensive tactics your team is likely to face. We explain important attacking tactics and highlight specific player roles to help you select the best play and position key personnel.

Chapter 4 features 22 plays, plus variations on those plays to provide excellent options for any corner-kick situation. The country's top soccer programs use these plays when they want to score a corner-kick goal. Use the helpful instructions and detailed diagrams to teach your team the plays. Add practice, and soon you'll be adding up the goals.

Corner Kick Tactics

Corner kicks offer great scoring opportunities because the ball is in the attacking third of the field and a goal can be scored directly from a corner kick. A member of the attacking team takes a corner kick to restart play after a defending player has put the ball completely over the goal line—but not between the goal posts—either in the air or on the ground.

Rules for the Corner Kick

The attacking team restarts play by taking a kick from within the quarter circle at the nearest corner flag post. The corner flag may not be removed during the corner kick. Defenders may not approach within 10 yards of the ball until it's in play, meaning that it has traveled the distance of its own circumference; if they do, the kick is retaken.

The kicker may not play the ball again until it has been touched or played by another player. This rule holds even if the ball hits the goal post and rebounds toward the kicker.

Defensive Tactics

Many goals are scored from corner kicks, so it is essential for the defense to be organized. As with free kicks, the coach must understand general defensive tactics and the opponent's specific strengths and weaknesses, and utilize this information effectively in the team's practice sessions.

When the attacking team is awarded a corner kick, the defending team will probably have most of its players in its defensive third of the field, and they should move quickly to prearranged positions. Two defensive players take positions near the far post—one to protect the space behind the goalkeeper, the other to cover an attacker who has occupied or is attempting to occupy vulnerable space in front of the far post. Another defender covers the near post to clear a short kick from the goal area or to pass the ball to a teammate. The goalkeeper sets up near the middle of the goal to intercept a long cross or move along the goal line or out from it to catch or clear balls swinging in toward the goal. If the ball can't be caught, the goalkeeper must punch or tip it completely over the goal and out of play. A defender should be 10 yards from the player taking the corner kick to distract the kicker and to be in position to intercept an errant cross or a pass to a nearby attacker. This defender can be in a position that encourages either a low inswinger or outswinger and, if such a kick is taken, moves laterally to block the ball. On short corners, a defender must oppose the extra player to keep equality in numbers. Other defensive players mark attacking players who have moved or may move to scoring positions. Midfielders and forwards on the defensive team may have to move into the defending area if the attacking team brings more players up.

Alertness and communication are essential to avoid breakdowns. The goalkeeper must shout clear and timely instructions. The goalkeeper and defenders must get to the ball as high as possible in its flight. Leaving space open and playing the ball below head-height invites disaster. All defenders move out of the area immediately on a clear or pass. The defense tries to create depth by positioning players from the goal line out to the middle third of the field so that a defender can clear or pass the ball immediately upfield to a teammate. Absence of depth may limit defenders to making short passes in confined areas, aiding attackers in regaining ball control.

Attacking Tactics

The coach must utilize the team's offensive strengths and exploit the opponent's defensive weaknesses. The coach wants to know

- whether the opponent covers the posts,
- where the goalkeeper usually stands,
- whether the other defenders mark players or space,
- whether the defense is alert, with good communication between the goalkeeper and all defenders,
- whether the goalkeeper comes out or stays in the goal,
- whether the goalkeeper tries to catch difficult balls or punches them,
- whether a defender comes out to the wing to counteract a short corner play,
- whether other defenders come back quickly or at all to cover extra attackers,
- whether the defenders are good headers and clear the ball effectively,
- whether the defenders leave space open or play the ball below head-height, and
- whether they move out quickly after a clear.

The attacking team enjoys the advantage of the opportunity to execute well-rehearsed restart plays near the front of the goal. Greater risk than usual may be taken in its attacking third of the field because even if the defenders gain possession of the ball, they must advance it almost the entire length of the field to create a scoring opportunity of their own. All attacking players except the goalkeeper have a role in the corner kick play. The coach must identify players who can deliver accurate inswinger and outswinger corners. Key players are carefully selected for their heading ability. One of these players sets up at the near post, one in front of the goalkeeper, and two outside the far post. Two or three other attackers may be brought up if needed. Extra attackers brought into the area create physical and psychological pressure on the defense.

The attacker taking the corner kick gives the signal by word or physical action to start the play. On the kick, the near-post attacker moves toward the ball, trying to be the first one there and to make the first touch on goal or across the goal. Players in the middle of the area are alert for a flick-on pass, and the attackers outside the far post move to lose their markers and be in position to attack the ball. Players outside the edge of the penalty area stay ready for a pass or weak clear. The other attackers are alert and prepared to react to a quick counterattack by the defending team.

A primary tactic on corner kick plays is for the attackers to move aggressively to get goal-side and be first to the ball. There can be no better example of the importance of this tactic than France's first two goals from corner kicks in their defeat of Brazil in the World Cup '98 championship game. Taking the ultimate advantage of Brazil's defensive weakness, Zinedine Zidane scored twice by making aggressive runs, eluding his marker, being first to the ball, and heading two brilliant shots into the goal.

The power of a shot taken on goal is not as important as being first to the ball and directing it to an open area. The odds of scoring at the far post are not as good as at the near post or in the central area. On far-post corner kicks, the ball is in flight longer, giving defenders more time to be first to the ball and clear it. The best play is an inswinger aimed at the front of the goal area. Such a goal was scored by an attacker in Nigeria's 3-2 World Cup '98 win over Spain. Another tactic is for the near-post or other attacker to run to the corner to draw a defender and create open space for other attackers. Croatia won a 1-0 World Cup '98 game over Jamaica on a short corner kick play. A Croatian attacker, after receiving a short pass from the corner kicker, turned and centered the ball to the near-post attacker, who flicked the ball on to an unmarked Mario Stanic in the central area for the winning goal. A corner kick play that capitalized on the heading strength of the attackers and the defenders' failure to closely mark those in the key central area took place in the World Cup '98 game between Germany and the United States. A long corner kick was made to the far-post area, where a German attacker out-headed the U.S. defenders and redirected the ball back to the central area. Oftentimes, such a pass catches the defenders with their attention and response still focused on the initial pass. It worked this time as an unmarked Andy Moller headed the ball into the goal at the near post for Germany's first score in its 2-0 win.

Corner Kick Plays

Select a few of these 22 corner kick restart plays to rehearse and use in game situations. They can be made nearly perfect through practicing proper technique, communication, movement, and timing.

The coach, or the player taking the corner kick, will determine the play to be executed. You can use the following factors to choose the appropriate play:

- Defensive positions assumed by the opposing players
- Environmental conditions such as high wind, which may prompt the kicker to elect to keep the ball low or make a short pass, or slippery conditions, which may suggest that the kicker take a direct curved shot on goal
- Strengths and weaknesses of both attackers and defenders

As noted in chapter 3, the keys to a successful free kick include players' being organized, knowing and following their roles, moving aggressively to get goal-side, being first to the ball, drawing defenders away to create open space, and being alert for a pass or weak clear.

Attack

Formation

Attacker 1 is in position to take the corner kick. Attackers 2 and 3 are in the middle of the goal area. Attacker 4 is at the edge of the attacking third of the field, 10 yards in from the near sideline. Attackers 5, 6, and 7 are spread out inside the far corner of the penalty area. Attackers 8 and 9 are outside the near and far corners, respectively, of the 18-yard line.

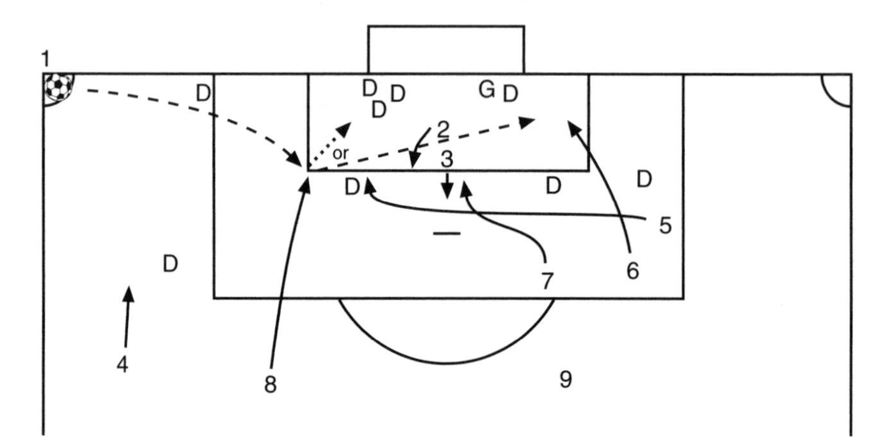

Procedure

As soon as 1 gives the predetermined signal, 2 and 3 check to the six-yard line. 4 makes a delayed run toward the goal line. 5, 6, and 7 make delayed sprints to cover the near-post corner, far-post corner, and middle of the goal area, respectively. 1 makes an outswinger or inswinger corner kick to 8, who has sprinted toward the near corner of the goal area. 8 takes a first-time shot on goal or flicks the ball to the far post to 6, who takes a shot on goal. All other players stay alert for a possible rebound.

Variation

As soon as 1 gives the predetermined signal, 2 and 3 check to the six-yard line. 5, 6, and 7 make delayed sprints to cover the near-post corner, far-post corner, and middle of the goal area, respectively. 1 passes to 4, who is making a delayed run toward the goal line. 4 either goes two on one with 1 or crosses to the far post to 6, who shoots on goal.

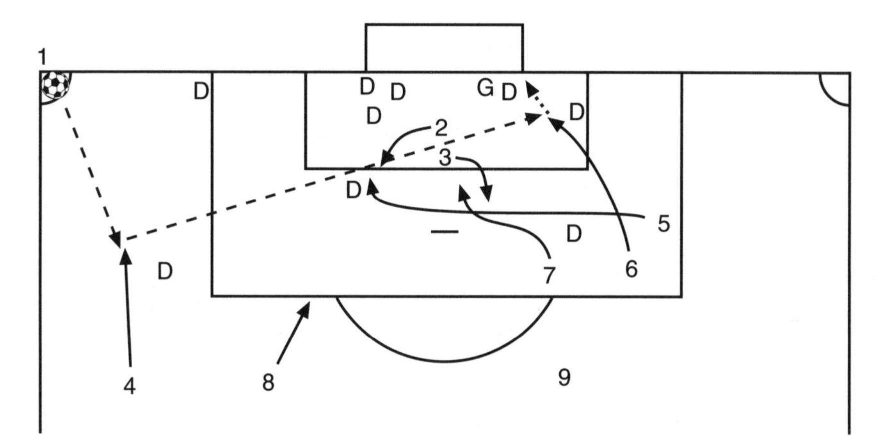

Defensive Tips

Communication and alertness are essential. A defender covers each post. Another stands on or near the goal line 10 yards from the kicker, alert and ready to block a low pass. Defenders playing the ball below head-height and leaving space open in the central scoring area invite trouble. The goalkeeper must punch the ball out of the area or completely over the goal if it cannot be caught.

Offensive Tips

An inswinger to the near post has the best chance of success, especially if there is no defender on the line 10 yards from the kicker, or the goalkeeper is short or plays the ball below head-height. Good decoy runs are essential to clear space for the primary attacker. 8's run and the timing of the pass to 8 are critical to the success of this play.

Contributor: Thomas R. Martin, Men's Coach, James Madison University, Harrisonburg, Virginia

Clock

Formation Attacker 1 is in position to take the corner kick. Attacker 2, preferably a tall player, is in the middle of the goal area. Attackers 3, 4, 5, and 6 are each in a different corner of the goal area. Attacker 7 is on the far sideline of the penalty area near the goal line.

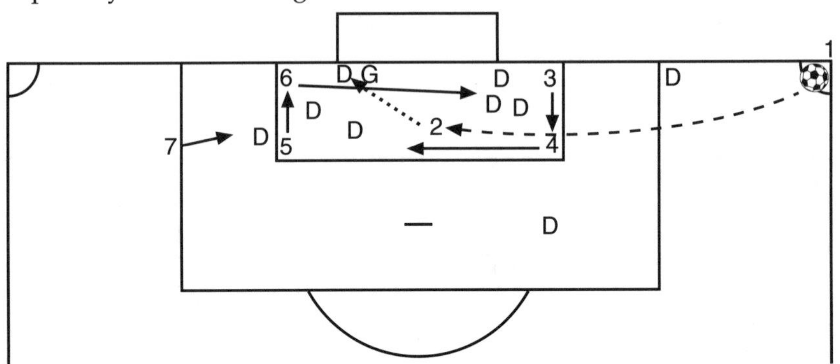

Procedure 1 initiates the restart by yelling "Clock!" 3, 4, 5, and 6 immediately move clockwise around the inside of the goal area perimeter, keeping the spacing of their initial positions. 1 makes a high corner kick to 2, who takes a first-time head shot on goal. 3, 4, 5, and 6 stay alert for a possible rebound. 7 stays alert for a long corner kick or a loose ball slipping through the goal area.

Variation The kicker yells "Counter!" and the players move in a counter-clockwise direction. The remainder of the play is completed as usual.

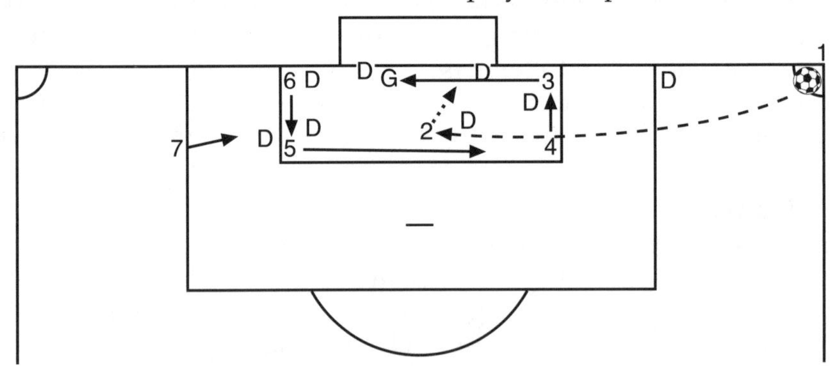

Defensive Tips A defender covers each of the posts. Another defender is on or near the goal line 10 yards from the kicker. All defenders must keep alert to prevent open space in the central scoring area. The goalkeeper must punch the ball out of the area or completely over the goal if it is difficult to catch.

Offensive Tips The attacking team can bring in extra players to intimidate the defense. It is important for 2 to be first to the ball and direct a shot to an open corner of the goal.

Contributor: Thomas M. Taylor, Former Boys' Coach, Hawthorne High School, Hawthorne, New Jersey

Corner Driven to Near Post

Formation

Attacker 1 is in position to take the corner kick. Attacker 2, preferably a tall player, is at the near post. Attackers 3, 4, and 5 stand along the top of the 18-yard line. Attacker 6 is just outside the 18-yard line on the same side as 1.

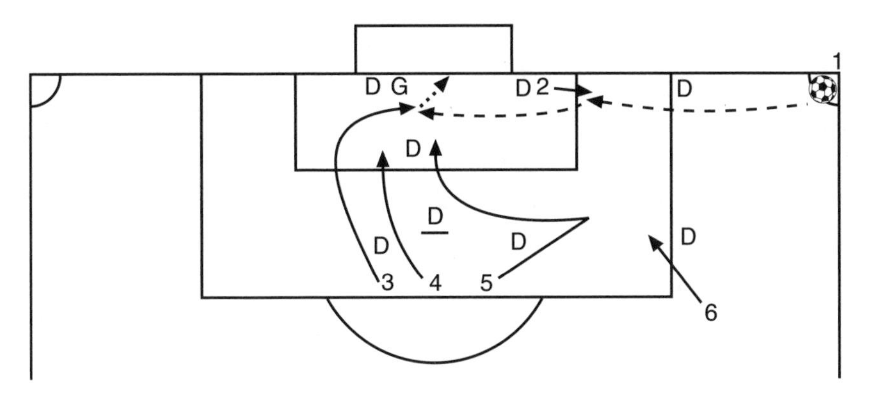

Procedure

On a predetermined signal, 3 makes a wide run past the far post toward the center of the goal area. 4 follows 3 and moves toward the far post. 5 checks toward 1 and then moves back toward the middle of the goal area. 6 moves to a position just inside the near sideline of the penalty area. 1 drives a head-high corner kick to 2, who moves toward the ball. 2 flicks the ball to the target area for 3, who takes a first-time shot on goal. All other players stay alert for a rebound.

continued

Corner Driven to Near Post *(continued)*

Variation

2, 3, 4, and 5 make the same runs. 1 drives the corner kick to 2. 2 heads the ball back to 6, who has moved into the penalty area. 6 crosses the ball to the far post to 4, who takes a first-time shot on goal. All other players stay alert for a rebound.

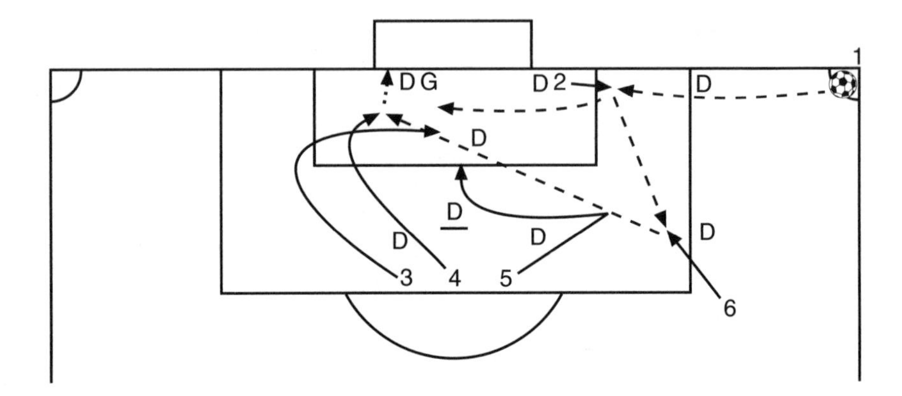

Defensive Tips

A defender is at each post. Another is on or near the goal line 10 yards from the kicker to clear a low pass and to prevent a short corner play. Players defending against 3, 4, 5, and 6 prevent them from getting goal-side. The goalkeeper and defenders play the ball as high as possible.

Offensive Tips

2 moves aggressively to be first to the ball. 4 and 5 make runs to distract defenders and open space for 3 in the central scoring area. 3 must be first to the ball and direct the shot on goal to an open corner.

Contributor: Diane R. Boettcher, Women's Coach, Middlebury College, Middlebury, Vermont

Corner One

Formation

Attacker 1 is in position to take the corner kick. Attackers 2 and 3 are on the far sideline of the goal area. Attackers 4, 5, and 6 are in a line 15 yards from the goal line and parallel to the 18-yard line.

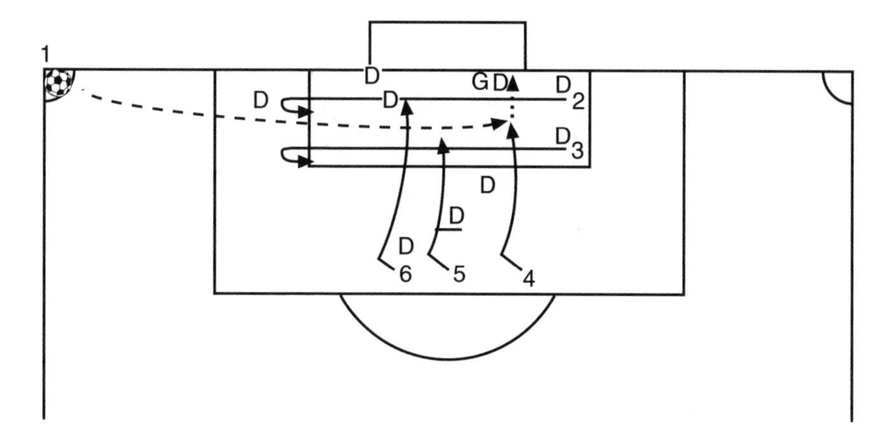

Procedure

To initiate the restart play and to distract the goalkeeper and defenders, 2 and 3 sprint across the goal area and curl back once they reach its near sideline. 4, 5, and 6 check in the direction of 1 and then curl back toward the goal area—4 toward the far post, 5 to the middle, and 6 toward the near post. 4, as the main target, must make an effective feinting move to get open. 1 counts one second and makes the corner kick to 4, who takes a first-time shot on goal. All other attackers stay alert for a possible rebound.

continued

Variation

2 and 3 make the same runs. 4 and 5 check in the direction of 1. 4 then cuts to the right side of the goal area, and 5 cuts behind 4 and makes a far-post run. 6 moves forward toward the near-post area to be in position for a possible rebound. 1 makes the corner kick to 5 at the far post for a shot on goal.

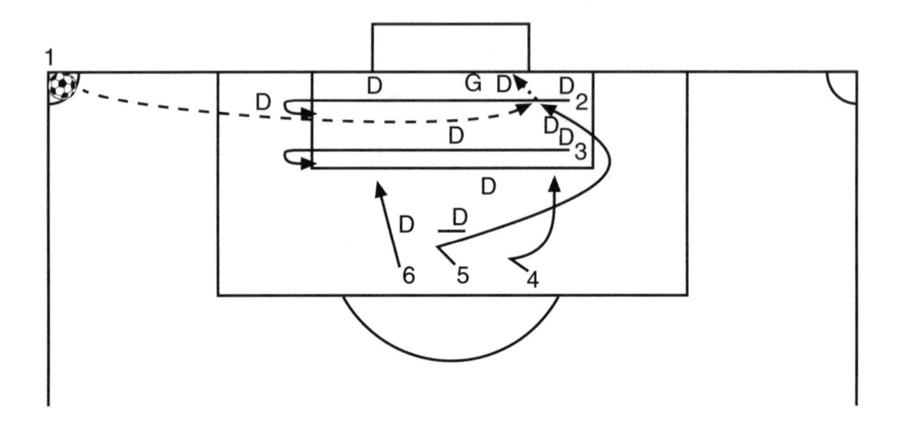

Defensive Tips

A defender is at each post and on or near the goal line 10 yards from the kicker. It is critical to play the ball as high as possible and clear it the first time. The goalkeeper must punch the ball out of the area or tip it completely over the goal if it cannot be caught.

Offensive Tips

Effective decoy runs are needed to draw defenders away from the primary target. If the goalkeeper does not come out of the goal area, or if a defender is not on the goal line, 1 can make a low pass to the near post for 6, who becomes the primary target.

Contributor: George D. Danner, Boys' Coach, Griffin High School, Griffin, Georgia

Crash

Formation

Attacker 1 is in position to take the corner kick. Attackers 2, 3, and 4 stand along the goal line within the goal area. Attackers 5, 6, and 7 are on the six-yard line behind 2, 3, and 4, respectively. Attacker 8 stands on the goal line at the far post.

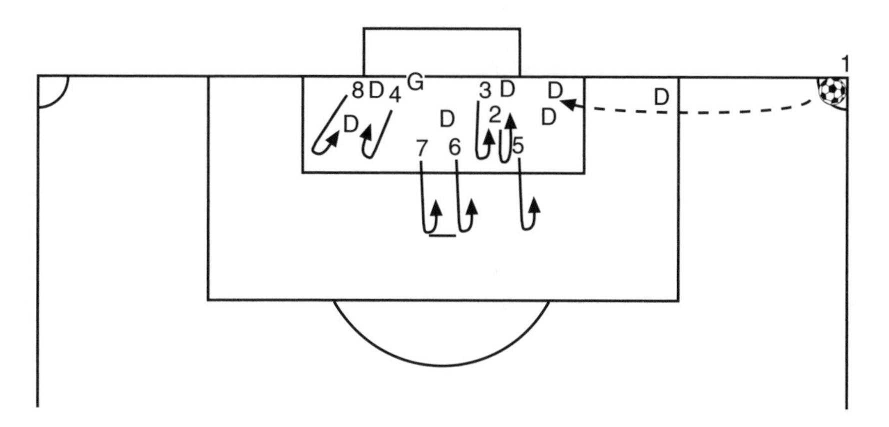

Procedure

On a predetermined signal from 1, all attackers check away from their initial positions and then "crash" back toward the goal area. 2, 3, and 4 check to the six-yard line and move back toward the goal line. 5, 6, and 7 check back until they are even with the penalty kick line and then move back toward the goal area. 8 checks toward the six-yard line and then moves back to the far post. As the attackers are moving back, 1 makes a hard-driven corner kick to the near post to 2, who takes a first-time shot on goal or flicks the ball on to the far post for any open player to shoot on goal.

Defensive Tips

A defender covers each post. Another defender is on or near the goal line 10 yards from the kicker, ready to clear a low pass. Other defenders must come back to pick up open attackers.

Offensive Tips

2 shoots on goal to the near post if the goalkeeper is not covering that post or flicks the ball on if the post is covered.

Contributor: Daniel Gilmore, Men's Coach, Rowan University, Glassboro, New Jersey

Double Stack

Formation

Attacker 1 is in position to take the corner kick. Two lines of three attackers each—attackers 2, 3, and 4 and attackers 5, 6, and 7—are at opposite sides of the penalty area.

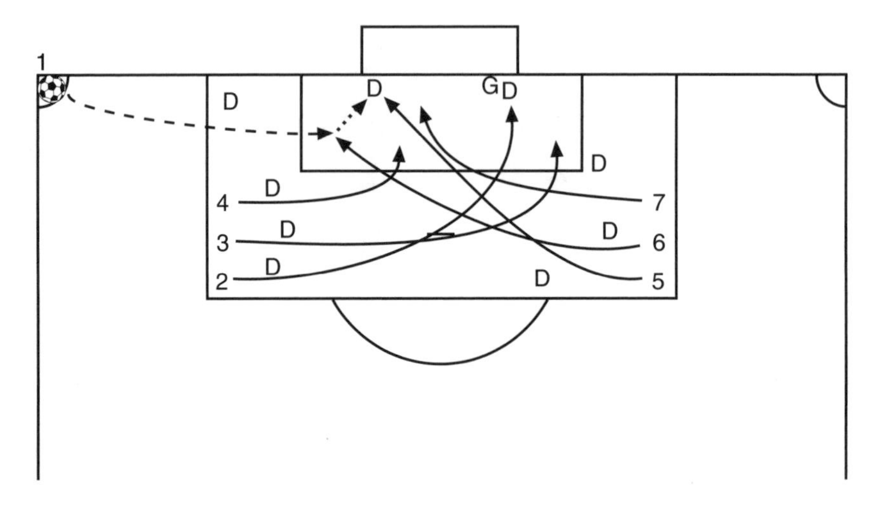

Procedure

Just before making the corner kick, 1 calls out a number from 1 to 4 to indicate where the ball will be kicked:

1-near post
2-far post
3-penalty line
4-center of goal area

The players in each line run toward predetermined positions:

Attacker 2-far post
Attacker 3-far-post corner of goal area
Attacker 4-middle of penalty area
Attacker 5-near post
Attacker 6-near-post corner of goal area
Attacker 7-in front of goalkeeper

The first player to get the ball takes a first-time shot on goal. All other players keep alert for a possible rebound.

Defensive Tips

A defender is at each post. Another is on or near the goal line 10 yards from the kicker. Extra defenders may need to come back to cover any open attackers. Those defending against 2, 3, 4, 5, and 6 must prevent them from getting goal-side.

Offensive Tips

The corner kicker should signal 1 if the goalkeeper is not known to come out of the goal or if a defender is not on the goal line 10 yards from the kicker. The signal should be 2 if the goalkeeper is short or the far post is not marked. 3 or 4 are appropriate signals if space is open in the middle area. All attackers must make aggressive runs to get goal-side and be first to the ball.

Contributor: Daniel R. Coombs, Boys' Coach, Loyola Academy, Wilmette, Illinois; Girls' Coach, Mother McAuley High School, Chicago, Illinois

Driven

Formation

Attacker 1 is in position to take the corner kick. Attacker 2, preferably a tall player, is at the near corner of the goal area. Attacker 3 is in front of the goalkeeper. Attackers 4 and 5 are at the far side of the penalty area near the 18-yard line. Attackers 6, 7, 8, and 9 are spread out in the attacking third of the field.

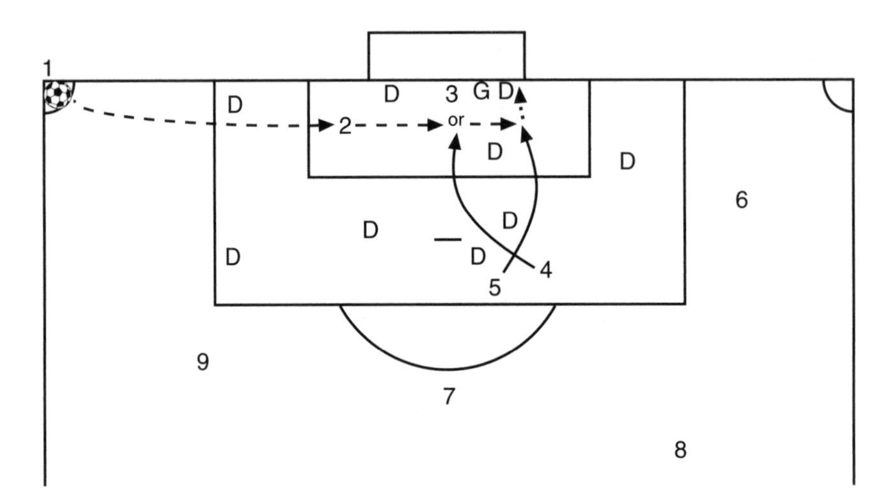

Procedure

1 makes the corner kick to 2. 2 flicks the ball on to 5 or 4, who have made crisscrossing runs to the far post and the middle of the goal area, respectively. Whoever gets the ball takes a first-time head volley shot on goal. 3 stays alert for a possible rebound. 6, 7, 8, and 9 maintain their positions, keeping alert for a possible long rebound or defensive clear.

Variation

1 makes the corner kick to 2, who lets the ball run through to 3 for a first-time shot on goal. To get into position for a possible rebound, 4 and 5 make crisscrossing runs to the midpoint of the 6-yard line and far post, respectively.

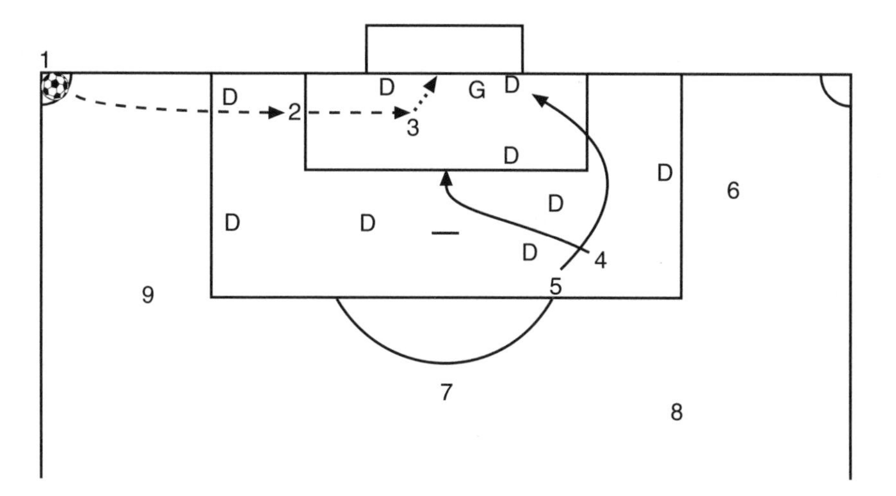

Defensive Tips

A defender is at each post. Another defender is on or near the goal line 10 yards from the kicker. Those defending against 4 and 5 must prevent them from getting goal-side. All defenders must be alert to prevent open space in scoring areas and must move to be first to the ball to clear it away.

Offensive Tips

It is essential to be first to the ball. If marked closely, 2 flicks the ball on. If not marked closely and if space behind is open, 2 dummies the ball through to 4 who is moving aggressively to the open space.

Contributor: Michael C. Mooney, Men's Coach, State University of New York College at Geneseo, Geneseo, New York

Flick On

Formation

Attacker 1 is in position to take the corner kick. Attacker 2 is two yards from the goal line and two yards from the near post. Attacker 3 is on the far side of the six-yard line halfway between the goal line and the six-yard line. Attackers 4, 5, and 6 are in a line along the six-yard line.

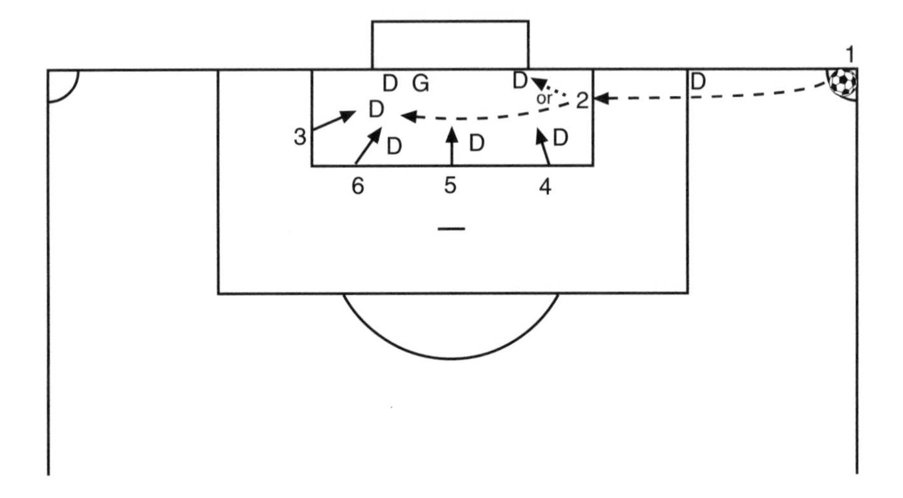

Procedure

1 plays an air ball to 2's head. 2 can flick the ball on to goal, to 3 at the far post, or to 4, 5, or 6, who moved into the goal area as 1 made the corner kick. All players stay alert for a possible rebound.

Defensive Tips

Defenders cover the near and far posts. Another defender is on or near the goal line 10 yards from the kicker. Those defending against 3, 4, 5, and 6 must keep them from being first to the ball.

Offensive Tips

2 shoots to the near post if the goalkeeper is not covering that post or flicks the ball on if the post is covered.

Contributor: John Makuvek, Athletic Director, Moravian College, Bethlehem, Pennsylvania

Heading Options

Formation

Attacker 1 is in position to take the corner kick. Attacker 2 stands on the center of the six-yard line. Attackers 3, 4, and 5 are in a line just outside the far corner of the six-yard line. Attackers 6 and 7 are on opposite ends of the penalty-area restraining arc.

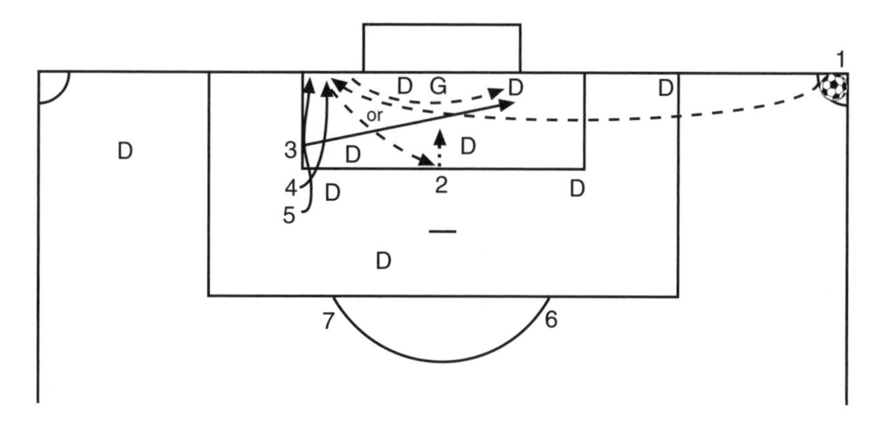

Procedure

On a predetermined signal from 1, 3 sprints to the near post, 4 runs to the goal line midway between the far post and the perimeter of the goal area, and 5 runs to the end line at the far corner of the goal area. 1 drives a high ball to 4, who makes a head pass either to 2 in the middle of the goal area or to 3, who has turned around at the near post to look for the pass. The player who receives the pass takes a first-time shot on goal. The other attackers stay alert for a possible rebound. 6 and 7 stay ready for a possible long rebound or defensive clear.

Defensive Tips

Defenders cover the near and far posts. A defender is on or near the goal line 10 yards from the kicker. Other defenders stay ready to come back and pick up extra attackers. Defenders must prevent attackers from being first to the ball and unmarked in the central scoring area. The goalkeeper must come out of the goal aggressively and play the ball as high as possible.

Offensive Tips

Attackers must make aggressive runs to be first to the ball. The first shot should be directed to an open post.

Contributor: George Perry III, Indiana Youth Soccer Coach, Indiana

In and Out

Formation Attacker 1 is in position to take the corner kick. Attackers 2, 3, and 4 stand two yards apart from each other along the six-yard line. Attackers 5 and 6 stand two yards apart inside the left side of the penalty line. Attackers 7 and 8 stand two yards apart inside the right side of the penalty line.

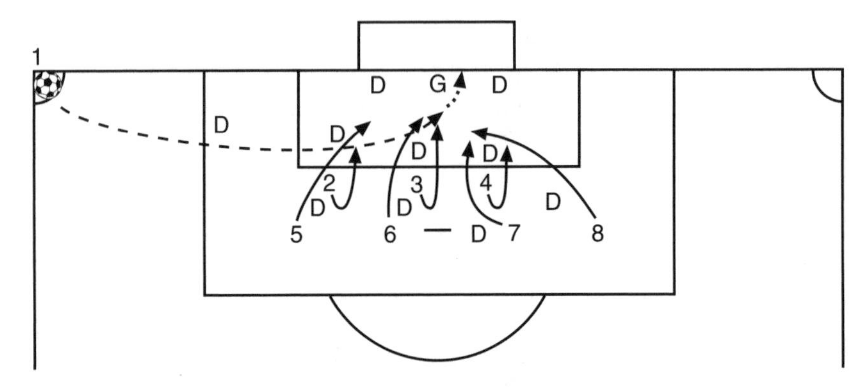

Procedure On a predetermined signal, the following happens simultaneously: 1 drives the corner kick toward the center of the goal area; 2, 3, and 4 take two steps out away from the 6-yard line and then immediately run back in toward the goal area; 5 and 6 run toward the far post; and 7 and 8 run toward the near post. The first player to get the ball takes a first-time shot on goal. All other players stay alert for a possible rebound.

Variation 1 On a predetermined signal, the following happens simultaneously: 1 drives the corner kick toward the center of the goal area; 2, 3, and 4 move away from the goal area and turn back to positions just outside the goal area; 5 and 8 make crossover runs toward the far and near posts, respectively; and 6 and 7 make straight runs to the near and far posts, respectively. The first player to get the ball takes a first-time shot on goal. All other players stay alert for a possible rebound.

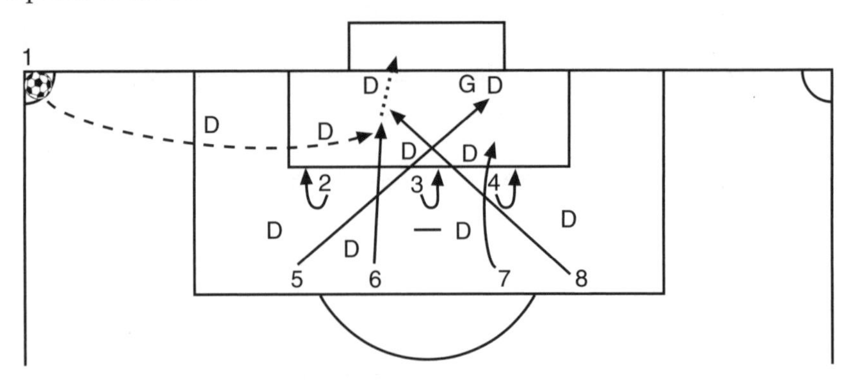

Variation 2

On a predetermined signal, the following happens simultaneously: 1 drives the corner kick toward the center of the goal area; 2, 3, and 4 move completely out of the penalty area and turn back to positions just outside the penalty area; 6 and 7 make crossover runs to the far and near posts, respectively. The first player to get the ball takes a first-time shot on goal. All other players stay alert for a possible rebound.

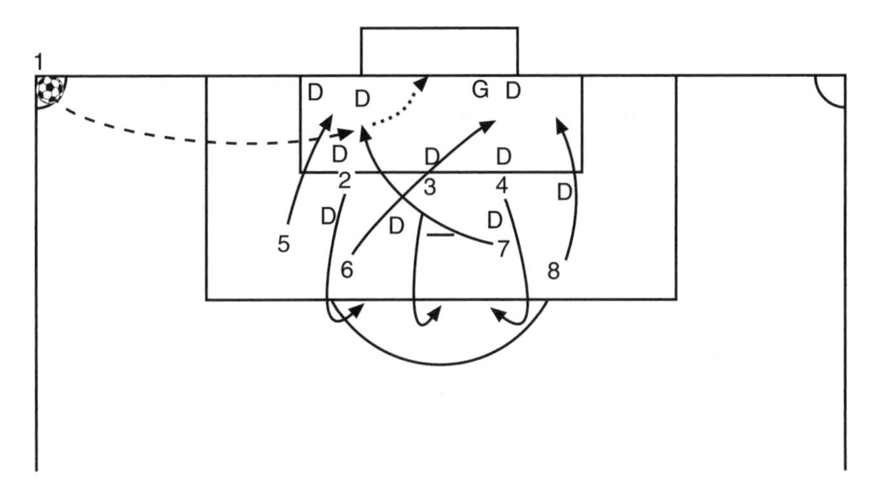

Defensive Tips

A defender is at each of the posts. Another defender is on or near the goal line 10 yards from the kicker. Other defenders must come back to pick up open attackers. The goalkeeper must be aggressive and get to the ball as high as possible in its flight. If the ball cannot be caught, the goalkeeper must punch it out of the area or tip it completely over the goal. All defenders move out of the area as soon as the ball is cleared.

Offensive Tips

The timing of each attacker's run is important. All attackers try to be first to the ball and direct the shot on goal to an open corner of the goal. All attackers challenge the defenders for rebounds.

Contributor: Stephen G. Scullion, Boys' Coach, Folling Community Club, Tyne and Wear, England

Lundy Skinner

Formation

Attacker 1 is in position to take the corner kick. Attackers 2, 3, 4, and 5 stand from left to right along the top of the 18-yard line. Attacker 6 is on the near-post sideline of the goal area. Attackers 7 and 8 are just outside the near and far corners, respectively, of the 18-yard line.

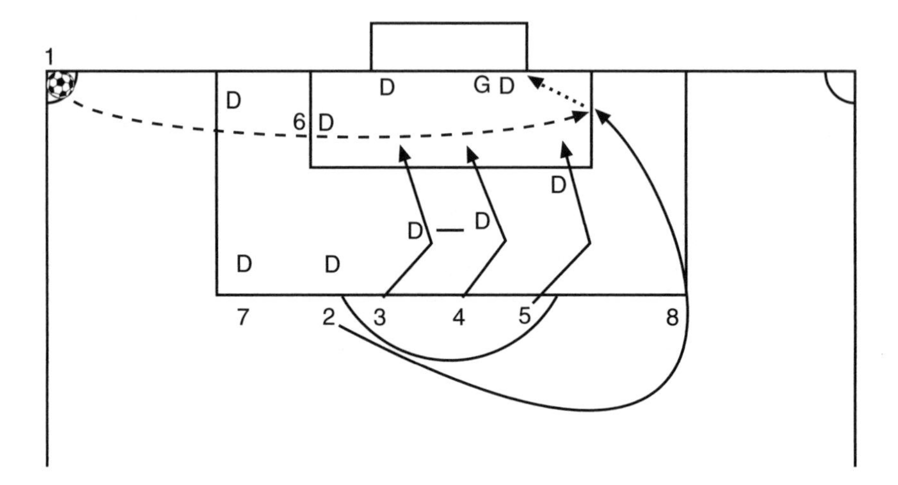

Procedure

After 1 gives a predetermined signal, 3, 4, and 5 check away from 1 and then sprint toward the near, middle, and far regions of the goal area, respectively. 2 cuts back around 8 and sprints toward the far post. 1 drives the corner kick to the far post to 2, who takes a first-time shot on goal or flicks the ball back toward the near post for any of the other attackers to shoot on goal. 7 and 8 maintain their positions and stay alert for possible defensive clears.

Variation

After 1 gives a predetermined signal, 3, 4, and 5 check away from 1 and then sprint toward the near, middle, and far regions of the goal area, respectively. 2 cuts back around 8 and sprints toward the far post. 1 makes a corner kick to 6, who flicks the ball on to 2 at the far post for a first-time shot on goal.

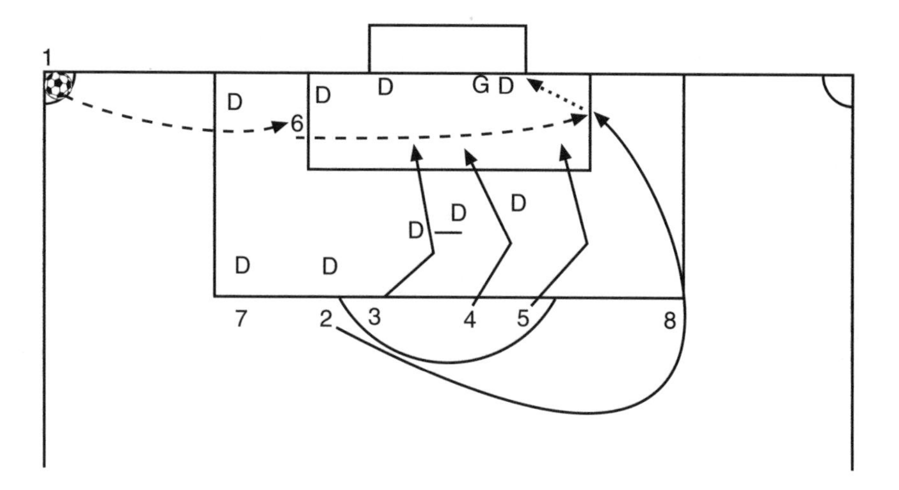

Defensive Tips

A defender is at each post. Another defender is on or near the goal line 10 yards from the kicker. Extra defenders will have to come back to cover open attackers. Defenders need to beware of losing concentration and leaving attackers open as the ball goes across the goal and back to the middle of the goal area.

Offensive Tips

3, 4, and 5 make their runs to distract the goalkeeper and defenders, and to create open space for the primary target. The player receiving the corner kick shoots on goal at the near post, or, if this post is not open, heads the ball to the opposite post.

Contributor: Bob E. Warming, Men's Coach, St. Louis University, St. Louis, Missouri

National

Formation

Attacker 1 is in position to take the corner kick. Attacker 2 is at the near post and Attacker 3 is at the far post. Attacker 5 stands at the penalty kick line. Attacker 4 stands in front of 5, a yard closer to the goal. Attacker 6, who should be a midfielder or fullback, is behind the corner of the 18-yard line on the same side of the field as 1.

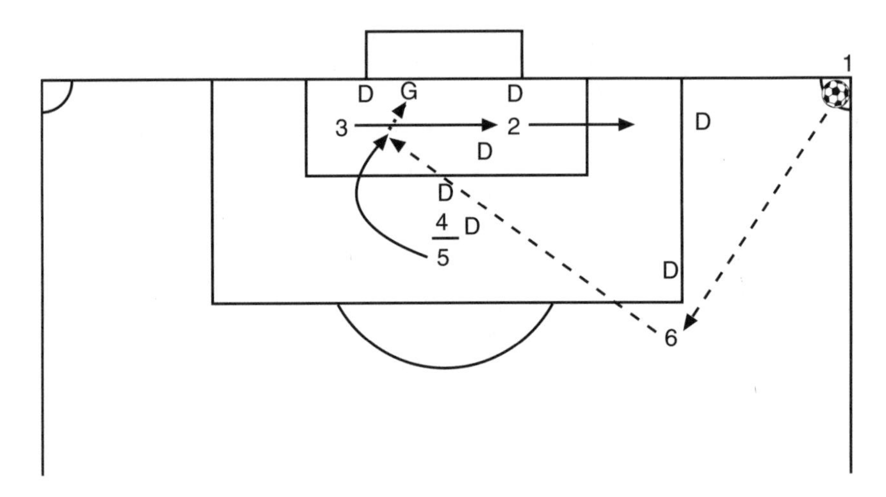

Procedure

As 1 moves toward the ball to take the corner kick, 2, calling for the ball, sprints toward 1. 3 moves across to the near post. 1 makes a well-paced ground ball pass to 6, who makes a one-touch pass toward the far post. 5, who has sprinted to the far post to receive the pass, shoots on goal. 3 and 4 stay alert for a possible rebound.

Variation

If the defense moves out of the penalty area on the pass from 1 to 6, 2 and 3 sprint away from the goal line to keep in onside positions. 4 and 5 move to the near post and far post, respectively, as 6 passes to either player for a one-time shot on goal.

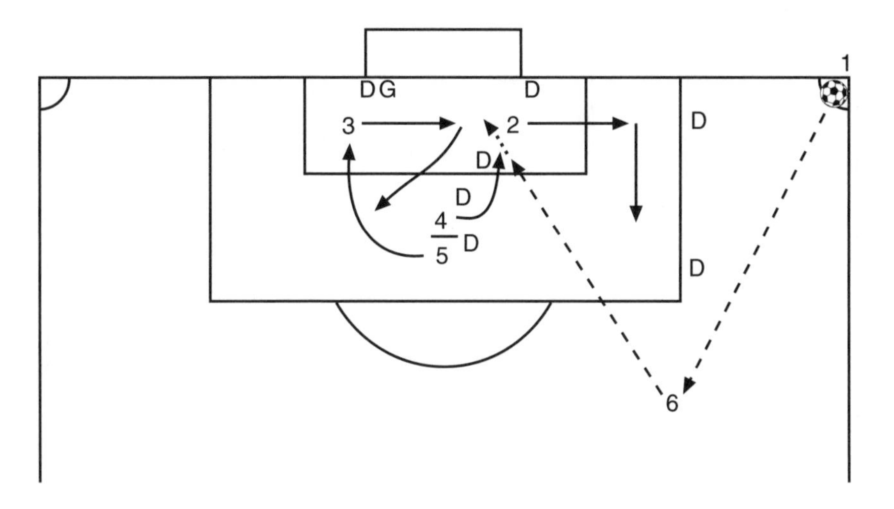

Defensive Tips

A defender covers each post, and another is on or near the goal line 10 yards from the kicker. A defender must move out with 2 to prevent a numerical advantage for the attack. A defender must come back to pick up 3 so that the far-post defender does not leave that area open. Those defending against 4 and 5 may have to switch so that 5 does not get goal-side.

Offensive Tips

The runs by 2 and 3 need to suggest they will be primary targets, which might open up space behind them for 5. In order for the pass from 6 to move in a downward arc, it should be made with the inside of the instep. 5 must make an aggressive run to be first to the ball and take a well-directed shot to an open corner.

Contributor: Helmut Werner, Men's Coach, Randolph-Macon College, Ashland, Virginia

Near or Far

Formation

Attacker 1 is in position to take the corner kick. Attackers 2 and 3 are at the near corner of the goal area. Attackers 4, 5, and 6 are next to each other at the far corner of the penalty area. Attacker 7 is at the midpoint of the penalty-area restraining arc.

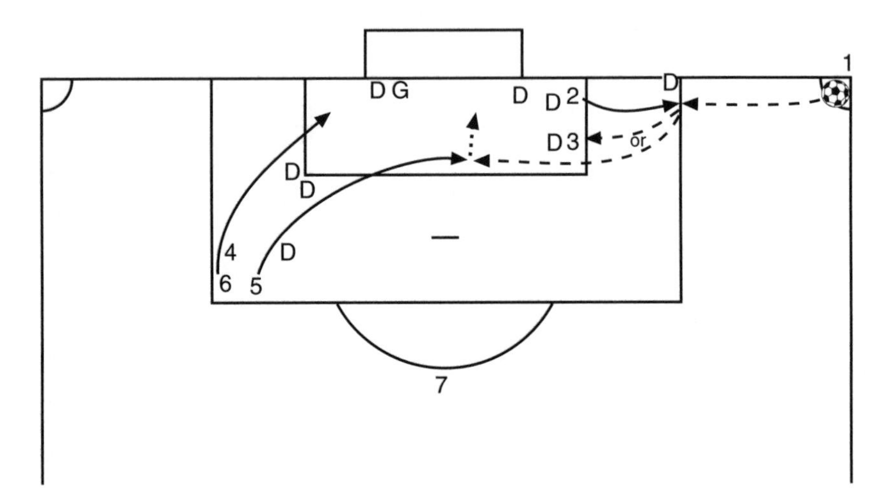

Procedure

On a predetermined signal from 1, 2 runs toward the near sideline of the penalty area. 1 makes the corner kick to 2's head. 5 sprints to the middle of the goal area, and 6 sprints toward the far post. 2 flicks to 3 or 5. Whoever gets the ball takes a first-time shot on goal. 6 stays alert for a possible rebound or a further flick from 5. 4 and 7 stay alert for a possible long rebound or defensive clear.

Variation

On a predetermined signal from 1, 2 runs toward the near sideline of the penalty area, 5 sprints to the middle of the goal area, and 6 goes toward the far post. 1 makes the corner kick to 3, who turns inside and shoots first-time on goal. All other attackers stay alert for a possible rebound or defensive clear.

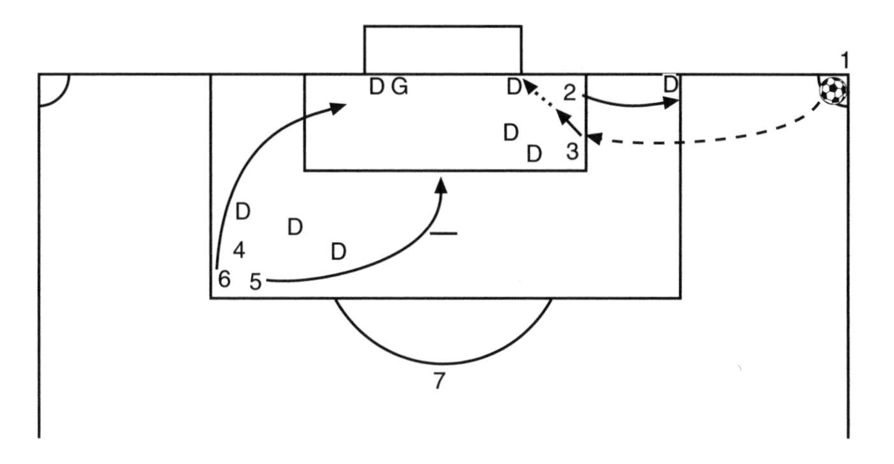

Defensive Tips

A defender is at each post. Another is on or inside the goal line 10 yards from the kicker. A defender must move out with 2 to prevent an easy short corner play. Those defending against 5 and 6 must move with them to prevent them from getting goal-side. The goalkeeper and defenders must move back quickly as the ball is flicked on.

Offensive Tips

2's runs are made to create open space behind him or her. If there is open space, 1 can make the pass directly to that area. If no space opens, the corner kick goes to 2 to flick on to 3 or 5.

Contributor: Jeffrey R. Tipping, Men's Coach, Muhlenberg College, Allentown, Pennsylvania

Open Up

Formation

Attacker 1 is in position to take the corner kick. Attacker 2 is in the center of the goal area. Attacker 3 is near the far corner of the six-yard line. Attacker 4 is on the penalty kick line. Attacker 5 is two yards outside the far corner of the six-yard line.

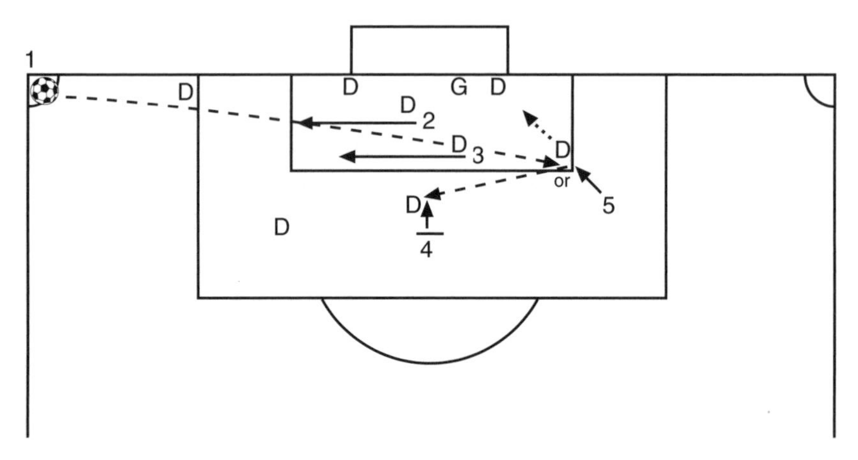

Procedure

After 1 gives a predetermined signal, 2 and 3 sprint toward the near sideline of the penalty area. 1 makes an outswinger corner kick to the far corner of the six-yard line to 5, who has timed a sprint to meet the ball as it gets to the corner. 5 either shoots first-time on goal or passes across the middle to 4, who has sprinted toward the goal from the penalty kick line to be in position to receive the pass and take a shot on goal.

Defensive Tips

A defender is at each post. Another is on or inside the goal line 10 yards from the kicker. Those defending against 2 and 3 must move with them. The defenders covering 4 and 5 must prevent them from being unmarked in the central scoring area. All defenders must try to be first to the ball and clear it from the area. The goalkeeper must play the ball as high as possible and punch it out of the area or completely over the goal if it cannot be caught.

Offensive Tips

To clear space behind them, 2 and 3 must make their runs look as though they are the primary targets. 4 and 5 make aggressive runs to be first to the ball. 5 takes a well-directed shot to an open corner or, if it appears space will be open in the central area, makes a pass to 4.

Contributor: Jay Martin, Men's Coach, Ohio Wesleyan University, Delaware, Ohio

Overlap

Formation

Attackers 1 and 2 are in position to take the corner kick. Attackers 3, 4, and 5 form a line parallel to the sideline near the far end of the 18-yard line. Attackers 6, 7, and 8 are spread out a few yards outside the 18-yard line from left to right, respectively.

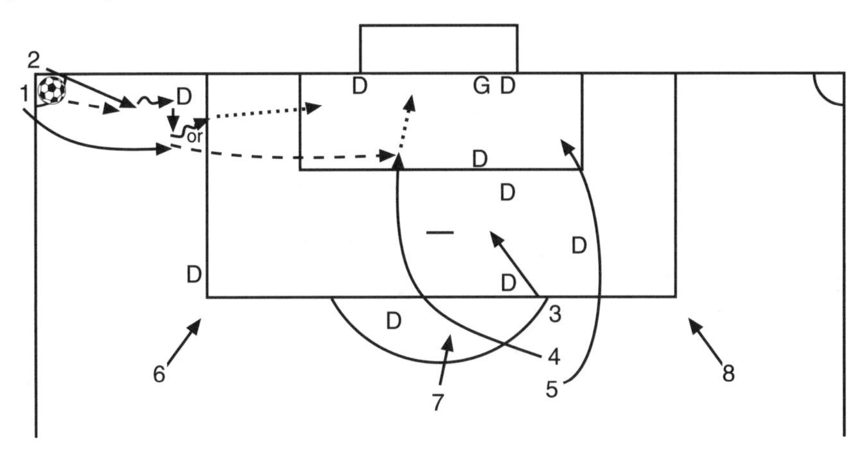

Procedure

1 initiates the play by tapping the ball forward to 2. 2 attacks and isolates a defender. 1 overlaps and receives a pass from 2. As 1 overlaps 2, 4 sprints toward the near post, 5 sprints toward the far post, and 3 sprints toward the penalty line. 1 either dribbles toward the goal and shoots to the near post or passes to 4, who takes a first-time shot on goal. 3 and 5 keep alert for a possible rebound. 6, 7, and 8, who have moved in toward the penalty area, stay alert for a possible long rebound or clear.

Defensive Tips

A defender covers each post. Another is on or inside the goal line 10 yards from the kicker. Another defender must move out to the corner to prevent a numerical advantage for the attack. Those defending against 3, 4, and 5 must stay with them to prevent them from getting goal-side. The goalkeeper must be aggressive and play the ball as high as possible. If it cannot be caught, the goalkeeper must punch the ball out of the area or tip it completely over the goal.

Offensive Tips

If a defender moves out of the goal area to cover the two attackers at the corner and leaves space open in the goal area, 1 can take a direct corner kick to 4 or 5 who are moving into the area. 3, 4, and 5 must make aggressive runs to be first to the ball.

Contributor: TJ Kostecky, Men's Coach, Long Island University, Brooklyn, New York

Peel Off

Formation

Attacker 1 is in position to take the corner kick. Attackers 2 to 7 line up on the penalty area sideline nearest 1, with 2 closest to the kicker. Attacker 8 stands 10 yards in from the near sideline and about 30 yards from the goal line.

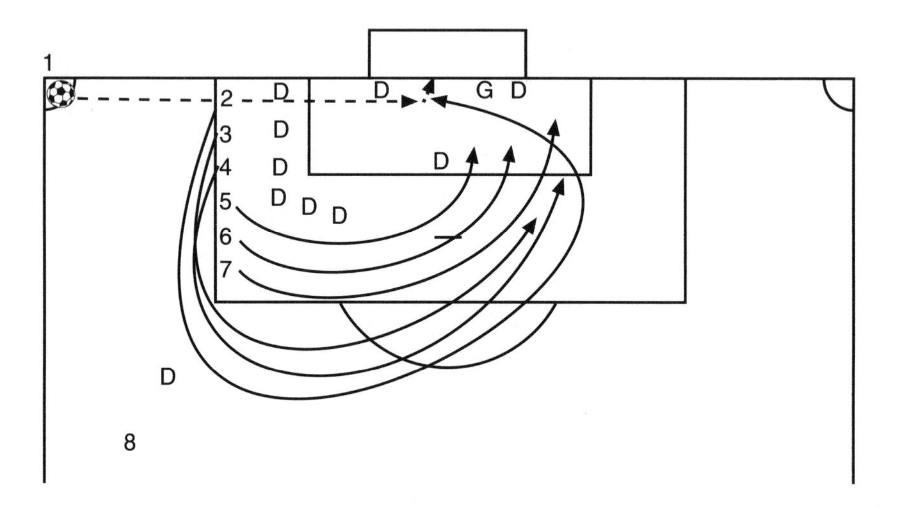

Procedure

On a predetermined signal from 1, the attacking players, beginning with 7, peel off one after the other and make bending sequential runs toward the far-post area. 2 continues on to the near-post area. 1 makes a low corner kick to the near post to 2, who shoots on goal. All other attackers stay alert for a possible rebound.

Variation

On a predetermined signal from 1, the attacking players, beginning with 7, peel off one after the other and make bending sequential runs toward the far-post area. 2 continues to the near-post area. 1 makes the corner kick to the far post or passes to 8, who crosses the ball to the far post. The first player to get the ball at the far post takes a first-time shot on goal.

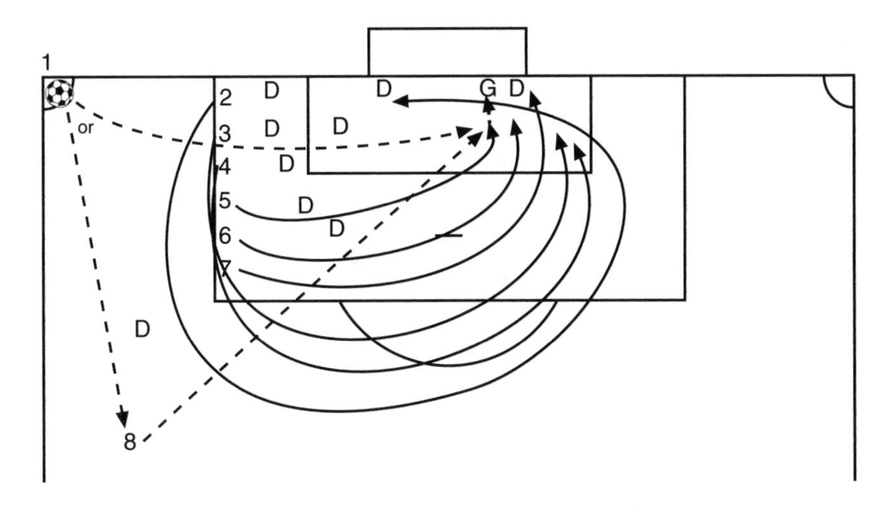

Defensive Tips

A defender is at each post, and a defender is on or inside the goal line 10 yards from the kicker. Other defenders must come back to cover any open attackers. The attackers must be marked and prevented from getting goal-side on their runs. Defenders, including the goalkeeper, must move aggressively to the ball and play it as high as possible in its flight.

Offensive Tips

Each attacker's run must be made as though that player will be the primary target. The attackers want to be first to the ball and take a well-directed shot to an open corner.

Contributor: C. Cliff McCrath, Men's Coach, Seattle Pacific University, Seattle, Washington

Shot

Formation

Attacker 1 is in position to take the corner kick. Attacker 2 is at the near-post corner of the goal area. Attackers 3, 4, 5, and 6 stand from left to right along the top of the 18-yard line.

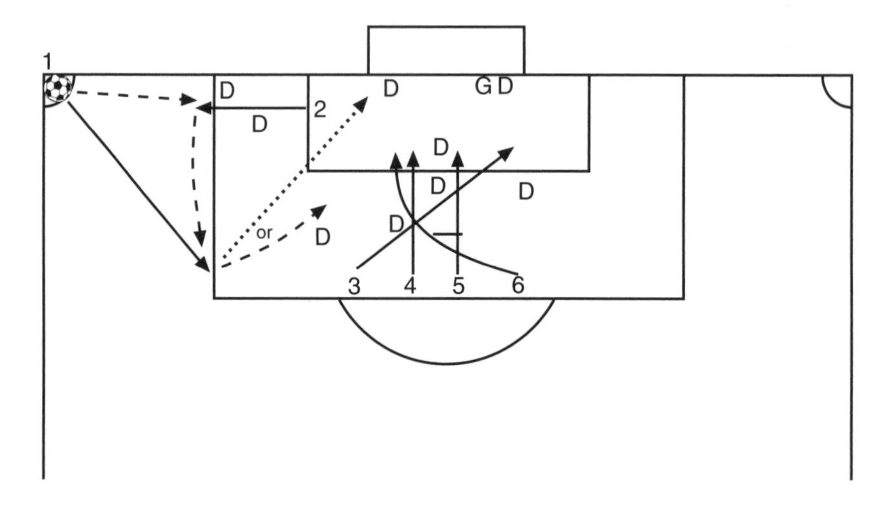

Procedure

1 initiates the corner kick by giving a predetermined signal to 2. 2 moves toward 1. 1 plays a short ball to 2 at the penalty area sideline. 1 follows the pass with a run toward the top of the penalty area sideline and receives a pass back from 2. As 2 makes the pass, the attackers on the 18-yard line sprint into the goal area, with 3 and 6 crisscrossing to the far and near posts, respectively, and 4 and 5 making straight runs. 1 either takes a shot on goal or passes to an attacker in the goal area, who takes a shot on goal. All other attackers stay alert for a possible rebound.

Variation

1 initiates the corner kick by giving a predetermined signal to 2. 2 moves toward 1. 1 plays a short ball to 2 at the penalty area sideline. If 2's defender is loosely marking or moves to cut off 2's pass to 1, 2 turns toward the goal line and shoots on goal or makes a short corner kick to the other attackers moving in on goal. The first player to contact the ball takes a first-time shot on goal. All other attackers stay alert for a possible rebound.

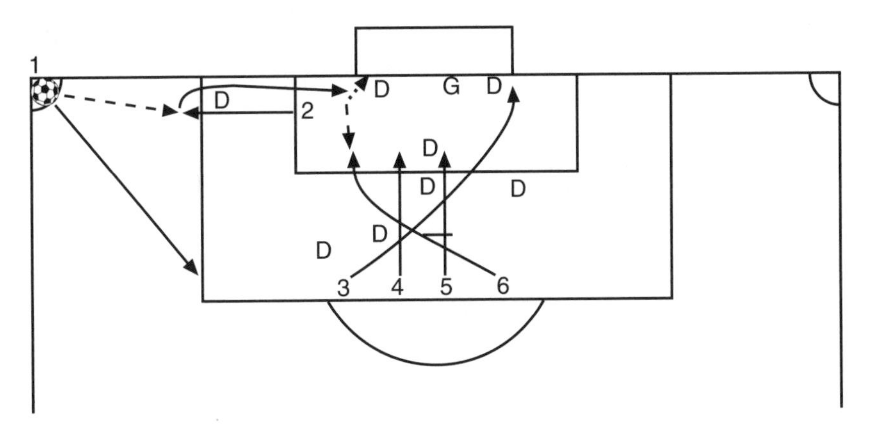

Defensive Tips

A defender is at each post. Another is on or near the goal line 10 yards from the kicker. A defender must move with 2 and the defender on the goal line stays with 1 following the pass to 2, preventing a numerical advantage for the attack. Those defending against 3, 4, 5, and 6 must prevent any of them from being first to the ball.

Offensive Tips

To beat the defenders and create open space, the runs and passes of 1 and 2 must be aggressive and crisp. 3, 4, 5, and 6 must move quickly to be first to the ball.

Contributor: Nick Mykulak, Men's Coach, Stevens Institute of Technology, Hoboken, New Jersey

Six

Formation

Attacker 1 is in position to take the corner kick. Attackers 2, 3, and 4 stand along the near-post sideline of the goal area. Attackers 5, 6, and 7 are in a line along the far side of the 18-yard line. Attacker 8 is 10 yards outside the far sideline of the penalty area and several yards in from the goal line.

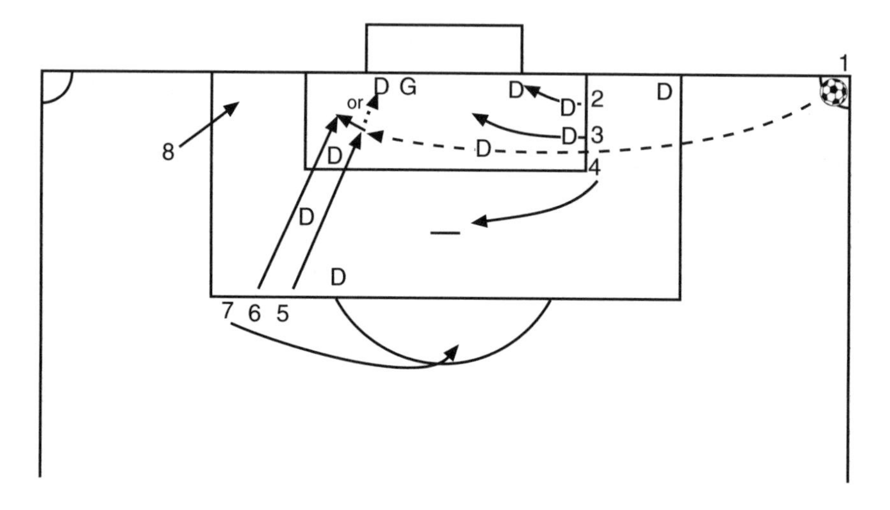

Procedure

The object of this restart is to get the ball to the feet of 5 or 6 at the far post. As 1 moves into position to take the corner kick, 2 cuts inside to the near post, 3 moves inside to the middle of the goal area, and 4 spins inside to the middle of the penalty area. As 1 makes a strong, low corner kick to the far post, 5 and 6 sprint toward the far post, with 6 just a few yards behind 5. 5 takes a first-time shot on goal and dummies the ball to 6, who shoots on goal. 2 and 3 stay alert for a possible short rebound. 7 and 8 move into position to be ready for a possible long rebound or clear.

Variation

2, 3, and 4 maintain their positions. 5 and 6 sprint toward the far post. 1 serves a head-high ball toward 2, 3, and 4, and one of them flicks the ball to the far post for a head shot on goal by either 5 or 6. All other attackers stay alert for a possible rebound or clear.

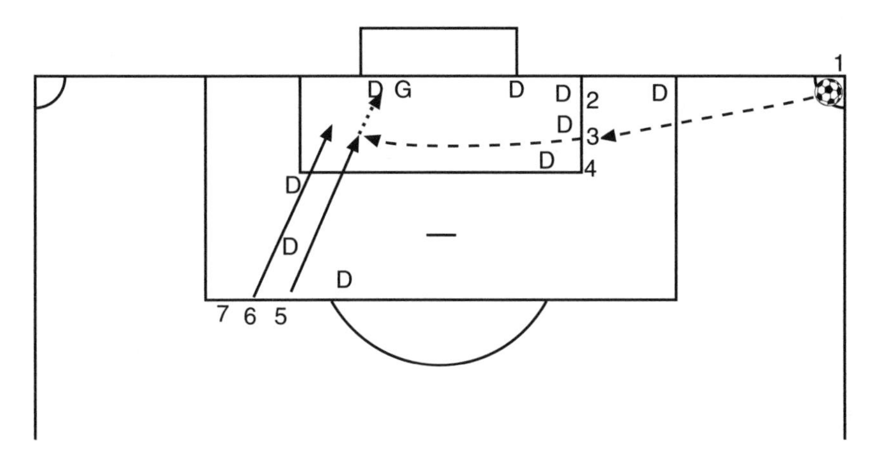

Defensive Tips

A defender is at each post. Another defender is on or inside the goal line 10 yards from the kicker. This defender moves to intercept a low corner kick. Those defending against 2, 3, 4, 5, 6, and 7 must prevent them from getting goal-side or being unmarked in scoring territory. Other defenders must drop back to pick up open attackers.

Offensive Tips

Well-timed decoy runs by the other attackers to clear space and confuse the defense are essential to the success of this restart play. 5 and 6 make aggressive runs to get goal-side and be first to the ball.

Contributor: Brian J. Woods, Men's Coach, William Paterson University, Wayne, New Jersey

Soccer Power Play

Formation

Attacker 1 is in position to take the corner kick. Attackers 2 and 3 are at the near and far posts, respectively. Attacker 4 stands a few yards outside the near corner of the penalty area. Attackers 5, 6, 7, and 8 are in echelon formation at the far corner of the penalty area. Attacker 9 stands 10 yards outside the midpoint of the penalty-area restraining arc.

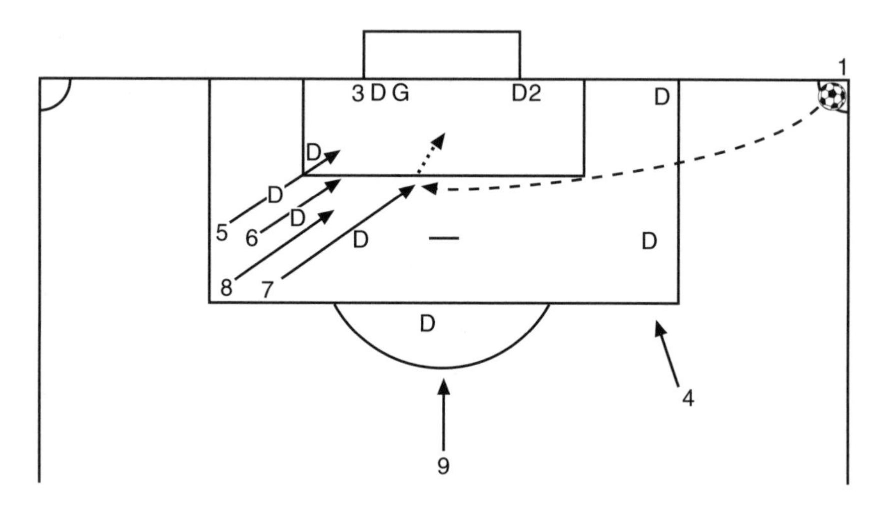

Procedure

As 1 attempts a seven-foot-high corner kick to an area two yards outside the middle of the goal area, 5, 6, 7, and 8 sprint toward the ball to get a first-time head or kick shot on goal. 2 and 3 stay alert for a short or long corner or rebound. 4 and 9 stay alert to redirect clears or rebounds back toward goal.

Defensive Tips

A defender covers each post. Another defender is on or inside the goal line 10 yards from the kicker. Those defending against 5, 6, 7, and 8 must prevent these attackers from getting goal-side and being first to the ball.

Offensive Tips

5, 6, 7, and 8 must make aggressive runs to get goal-side and be first to the ball. Pressure must be kept on the defense until the ball is cleared.

Contributor: John A. Reeves, Director of Physical Education and Intercollegiate Athletics, Columbia University, New York, New York

Stack

Formation

Attacker 1 is in position to take the corner kick. Attackers 2, 3, 4, 5, and 6 form a line parallel to the sideline in the center of the penalty area and face 1.

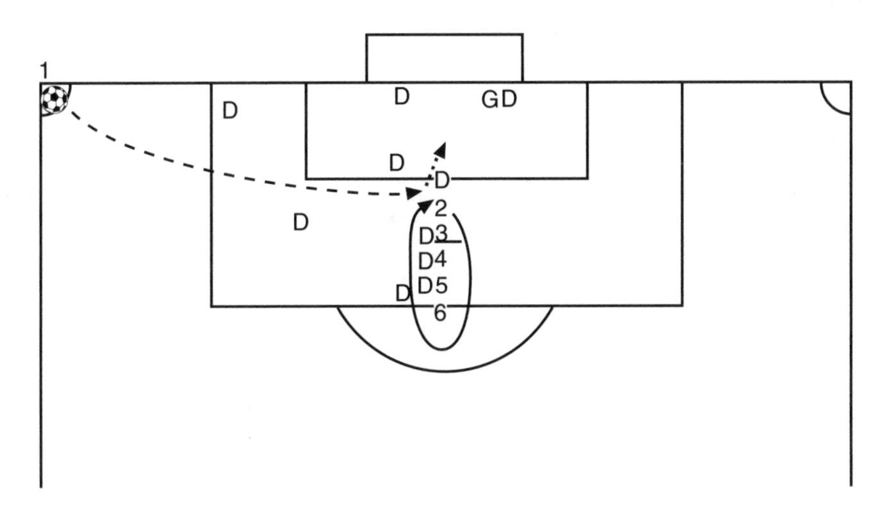

Procedure

2 initiates the restart by running around the end of the stack of attackers and then forward to meet the corner kick served by 1 toward the far post. 2 shoots on goal toward the near post.

Defensive Tips

A defender is at each post. Another defender is on or near the goal line 10 yards from the kicker. 2's defender must prevent the attacker from getting goal-side and being unmarked in scoring territory. Other defenders must stay alert to pick up coverage if 2 eludes the initial defender.

Offensive Tips

2's run must be close enough to the stack players to cause defensive confusion—and aggressive enough to be first to the ball. The other attackers follow up 2's run to be in position for rebounds. Attackers keep pressure on the defense until the ball is cleared.

Contributor: Susan M. Ryan, Women's Coach, State University of New York at Stony Brook, Stony Brook, New York

Tops

Formation

Attacker 1 is in position to take the corner kick. Attackers 2 and 3 stand shoulder-to-shoulder at the near post. Attacker 4 stands near the far sideline of the penalty area, and Attacker 5 stands inside the far top corner of the penalty area. Attacker 7 is a few yards behind 5 outside the far corner of the penalty area. Attacker 6 is at the midpoint of the penalty-area restraining arc.

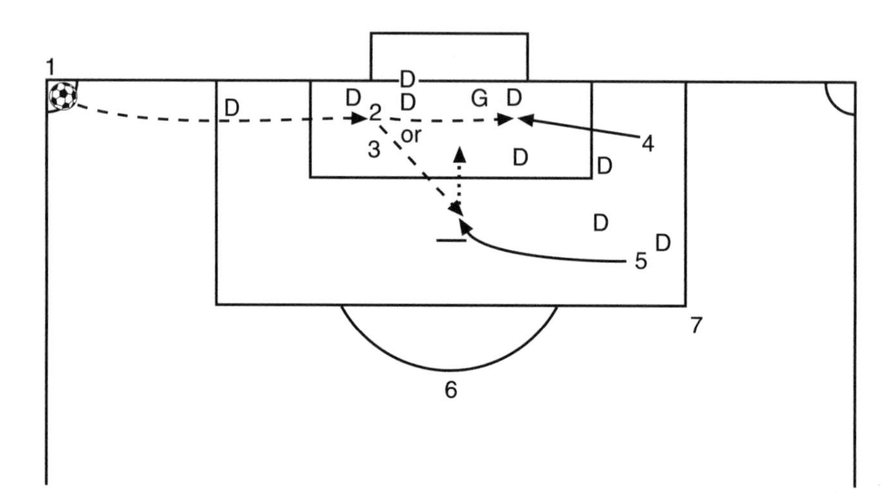

Procedure

1 serves a low, hard-driven ball to the near post. 4 runs to the far-post area, and 5 runs to the penalty line. 2 flicks the ball to either 4 or 5, and whoever gets it takes a head or volley shot on goal. 6 and 7 hold their positions outside the penalty area and stay alert for possible long rebounds or clears.

Defensive Tips

A defender is at each post. Another defender is on or inside the goal line 10 yards from the ball. The goalkeeper must catch the ball above head-height or clear the ball out of the area or completely over the goal line. Defenders must not let attackers get open in scoring territory.

Offensive Tips

4 and 5 must delay their runs until the kick is made to 2; then they make aggressive runs to get goal-side of their defenders.

Contributor: Vernon H. Mummert, Athletic Director, Wabash College, Crawfordsville, Indiana

Weak Side Stagger Runs

Formation

Attacker 1 is in position to take the corner kick. Attackers 2, 3, 4, and 5 are in a line on the far sideline of the penalty area. Attacker 6 stands on the penalty line. Attacker 7 is at the midpoint of the penalty-area restraining arc.

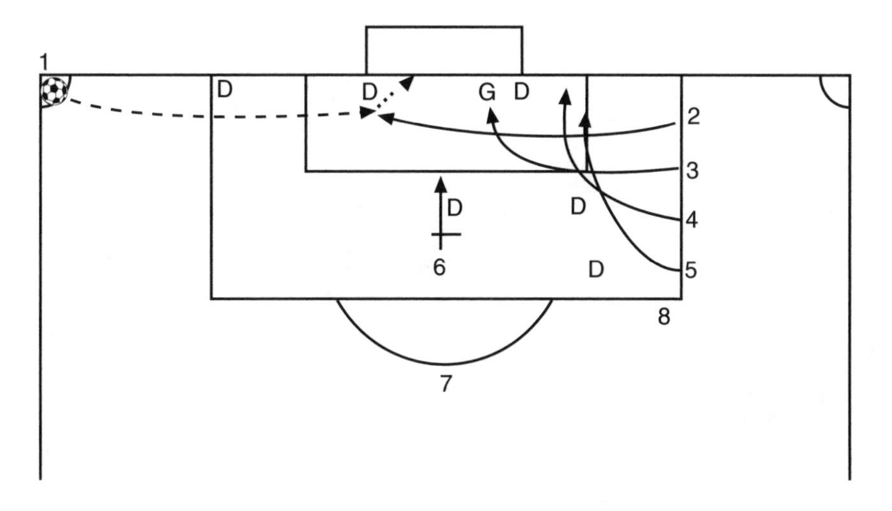

Procedure

On a predetermined signal from 1, the four attackers on the penalty area sideline, beginning with 2, make sequential runs to designated areas: 2 to the near post, 3 toward the goalkeeper, 4 to the far post, and 5 to a position in the far-post area just a few yards behind 4. 6 moves to the middle of the goal area. 1 drives a low corner kick, timing it to arrive at the near post at the same time as 2. 2 takes a first-time shot on goal. 3, 4, 5, and 6 stay alert for possible rebounds. 7 stays alert for a possible long rebound or clear.

Defensive Tips

A defender is at each post. Another is on or near the goal line 10 yards from the kicker. The defenders must communicate effectively to prevent losing their attackers. Other defenders must come back to pick up open attackers.

Offensive Tips

Timely runs by 3, 4, and 5 are essential to clear space for 2. 2's run must be aggressive to get goal-side and be first to the ball.

Contributor: Ted Eskildsen, Women's Coach, Mount Holyoke College, South Hadley, Massachusetts

Mark Thompson/Allsport

PART III

THE THROW-IN AND KICKOFF

As with the free kick and the corner kick, the throw-in and kickoff offer offenses opportunities to move into attacking positions either by exploiting a slow-reacting defense with a quick play or by moving to predetermined positions designed to gain a tactical advantage. Quickness is generally effective in throw-in plays, but there is obviously no need to rush the kickoff play.

In part III, we show you how to make the most of throw-in and kickoff plays. In chapters 5 and 7, we outline throw-in and kickoff rules and describe what kinds of defenses to anticipate. We discuss attacking tactics, including what roles your players might fill. In chapters 6 and 8, you'll find 12 throw-in and 10 kickoff plays, along with additional variations to strengthen your team's play in these situations.

Throw-In Tactics

The throw-in restarts play when the ball has gone out of bounds over a touchline (sideline).

Rules for Throw-Ins

A team takes a throw-in to return the ball to play after it has passed completely over a touchline. The thrower, when delivering the ball, must face the field of play, and part of each foot must be either on the sideline or on the ground outside the sideline. The thrower must use both hands equally, and must throw the ball from behind and over the head. The ball may be thrown in any direction. The throw-in is taken from the point where the ball crossed the sideline. The team that last touched the ball turns it over to the opponent for the throw-in, and any player on the team with possession can make the throw. The ball is in play as soon as it enters the field. A goal may not be scored directly from a throw-in. The thrower, as is the case with the kicker of free and corner kicks, cannot play the ball again until it has been touched or played by another player. If the ball is not properly thrown, the throwing team loses possession; the opposing team (which initially knocked the ball out of bounds) regains possession and takes a throw-in.

Defensive Tactics

A throw-in taken in the attacking half of the field is dangerous for the defense because the team in control of the ball may use a restart play and because a player cannot be offside on the throw-in. Attacking teams should use this danger to their advantage by having a repertoire of well-rehearsed restart plays. During a throw-in, defenders mark attacking players and space. Defenders in their defensive third of the field are particularly vulnerable to being beaten by a move to the ball followed by a sprint behind the defenders to space or to goal, and by a long throw to space when defenders are closely marking attackers. Even more dangerous to the defense is a throw to space directly in front of the goal.

Conversely, throw-ins taken in the attacker's defensive third of the field may provide the defensive team with a scoring opportunity if they regain possession of the ball in this area. In reality, the defense has a numerical advantage on the field because the attacker taking the throw-in is off the field. This advantage for the defense is even greater if the attacking team does not have a plan and/or the player taking the throw-in does not immediately get involved in the action on the field. Therefore, the attacking team must play with extreme caution in this area.

Attacking Tactics

With the exception of the conditions discussed in the defensive tactics section, the attacking team generally has a distinct advantage during the throw-in because it can use various plays, such as those in chapter 6. Attackers may move quickly toward the goal they are facing, while defenders have the disadvantages of retreating and having to anticipate the attackers' plans. Each attacking player has a role in the throw-in, such as receiving the ball from the thrower and then shooting or passing, or serving as a decoy to create space for another attacker.

The field position of the team taking the throw-in determines where to throw the ball. In the defensive third of the field, an attacker can throw the ball to the goalkeeper, who moves to the sideline of the penalty area to receive the throw-in. In the middle third of the field, the attackers can use designed plays involving throw-ins directly to various attackers or to predetermined spaces to which attackers are moving. Generally, it's best for the throw-in to go to the outside of the attacker, away from the defender. Because it's unusual for the defense to mark the attacker taking the throw-in, the attacker receiving the throw-in can return the ball quickly to the thrower. The thrower, who has immediately moved onto the field, continues the play by a short or long pass, or by dribbling the ball before playing it to another attacker. In the attacking third of the field, the attack can use plays similar to those used on corner kicks. This is particularly effective if the attack has one or more players capable of making long throw-ins.

Chapter 6

Throw-In Plays

A throw-in can be as effective a restart as a free kick or corner kick and should not be treated as just a method of getting the ball back in play. All players must keep in mind that every throw-in is an attack opportunity. Maintaining control of the ball is the main objective. If the attack does not have a plan, or if the throw-in is made carelessly, the attacking team will lose possession as often as it maintains it. Since a considerable number of throw-ins are taken in each game, practicing throw-in restart plays is time well spent. The 12 throw-in restarts in this chapter will provide you with an arsenal of plays to accommodate most throw-in situations.

Clear Space Into Space

Formation

Attacker 1 is in position to take the throw-in at midfield. Attacker 2 stands near the sideline, 20 yards closer to the goal line. Attacker 3 is square with 1 and 10 yards away from 1. Attacker 4 is behind 3 and 10 yards farther from the goal line.

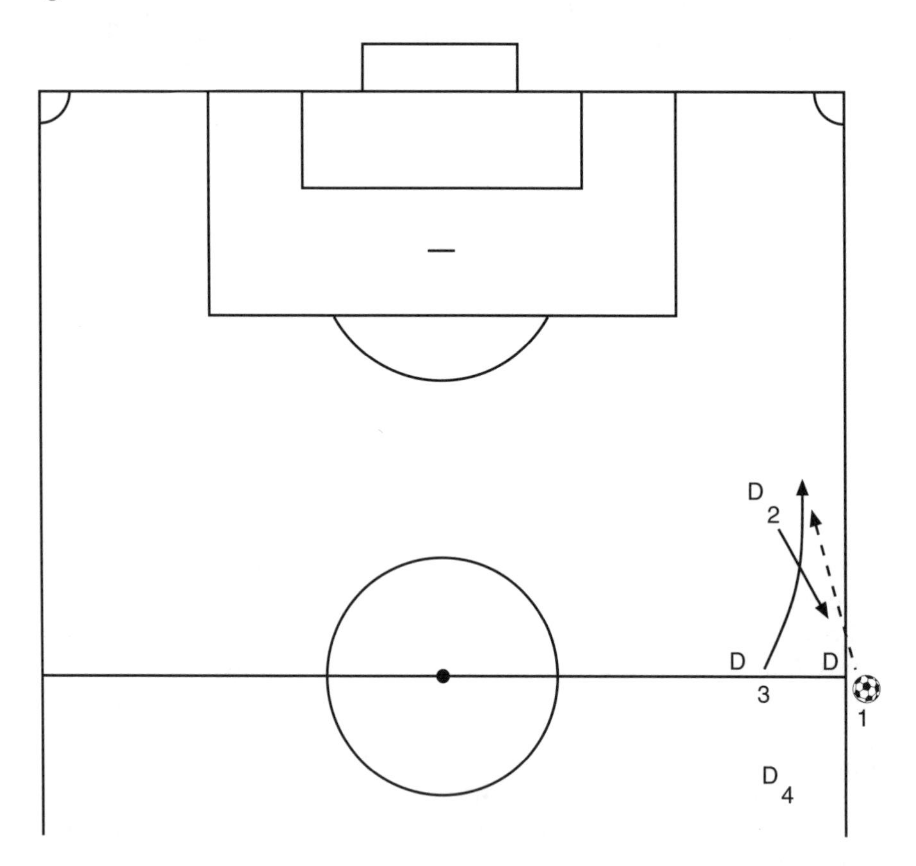

Procedure

2 initiates the throw-in by running toward 1. 3 sprints toward the space vacated by 2, timing the run to receive the throw-in from 1. 1 throws into the area between 3 and the sideline so that 3 can receive the ball on the run and shield it from the defender.

Variation 1

2 runs toward 1. 1 makes the throw-in to 2. If loosely marked, 2 turns with the ball and either moves up the field or passes to 3, who has run to the space vacated by 2. If tightly marked, 2 passes back to 1, who enters the field immediately after making the throw-in. 1 then passes the ball up the field to 3.

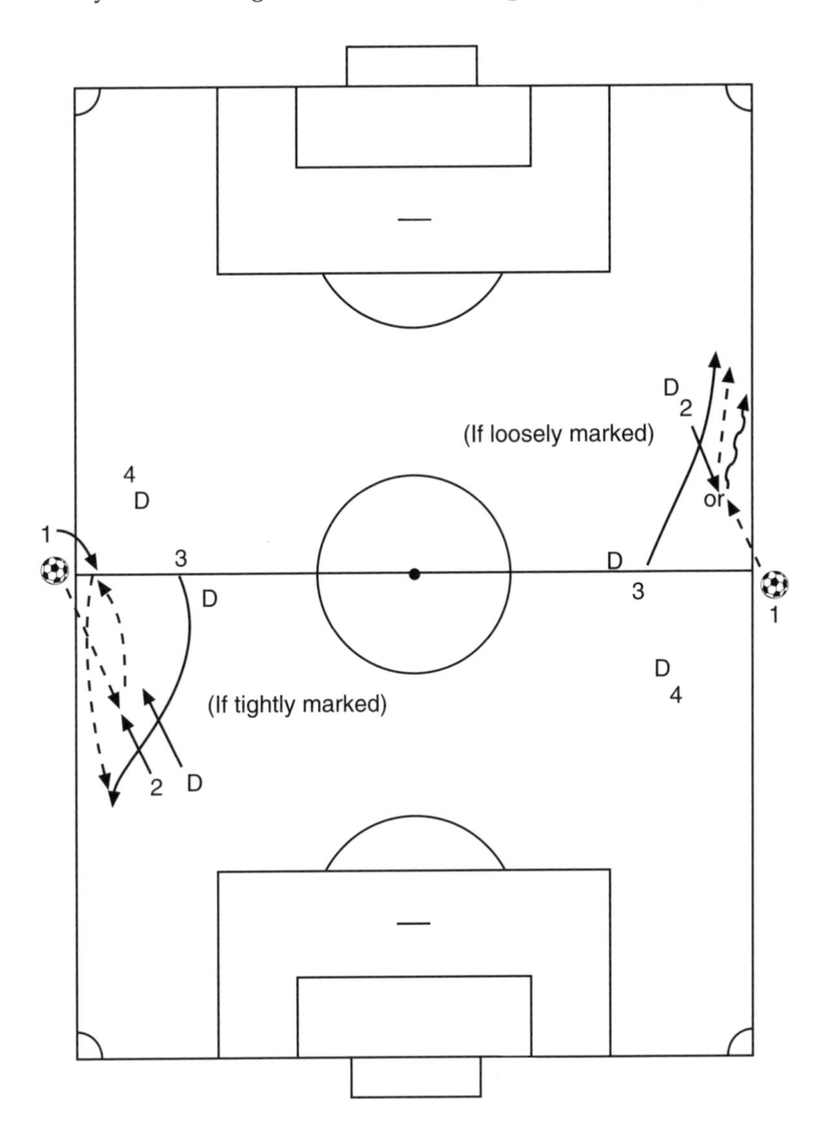

continued

Clear Space Into Space *(continued)*

Variation 2

2 runs toward 1. 3 runs to the space vacated by 2. At the same time, 4 runs to the space vacated by 3. 1 makes a square throw-in to 4, who moves up the field with the ball.

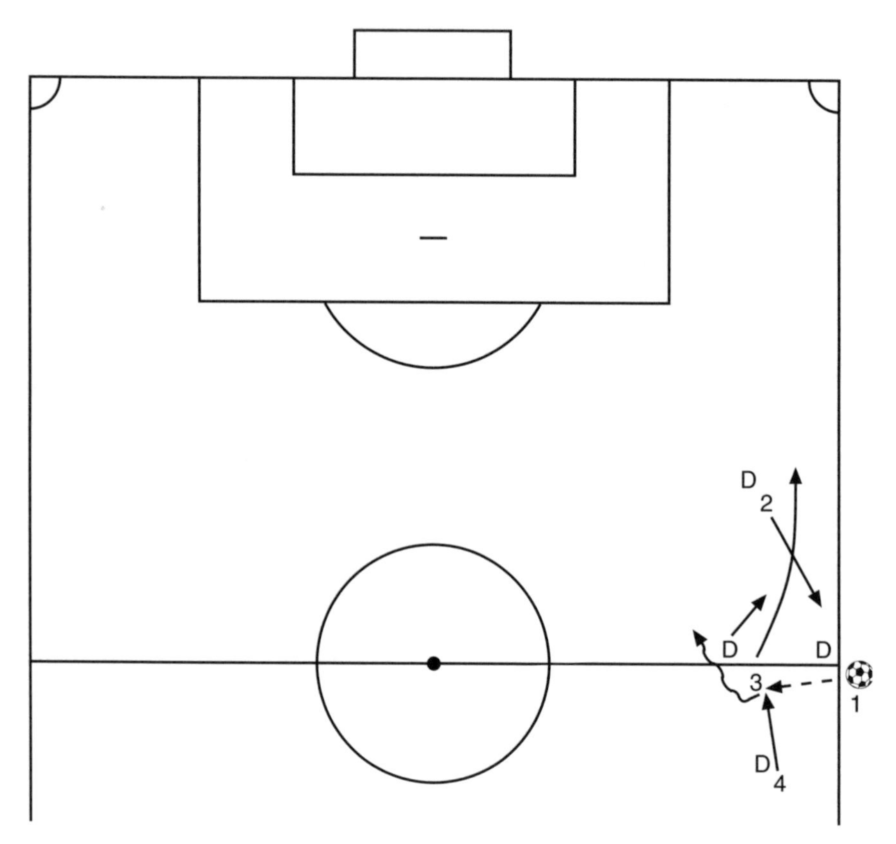

Defensive Tips

Defenders covering 2 and 3 must communicate with each other and possibly switch their coverage so that 3 cannot get goal-side.

Offensive Tips

The runs made by 2 and 3 are essential to the success of this play. 3 needs to run in front of the defenders so the throw-in from 1 will not be intercepted.

Contributor: Jay Gavitt, Former Assistant Boys' Coach, Columbia High School, Maplewood, New Jersey

Filler

Formation

Attacker 1 is in position to take the throw-in near midfield. Attackers 2, 4, and 6 and Attackers 3, 5, and 7 form two wide arcs, one behind the other, facing the player throwing the ball.

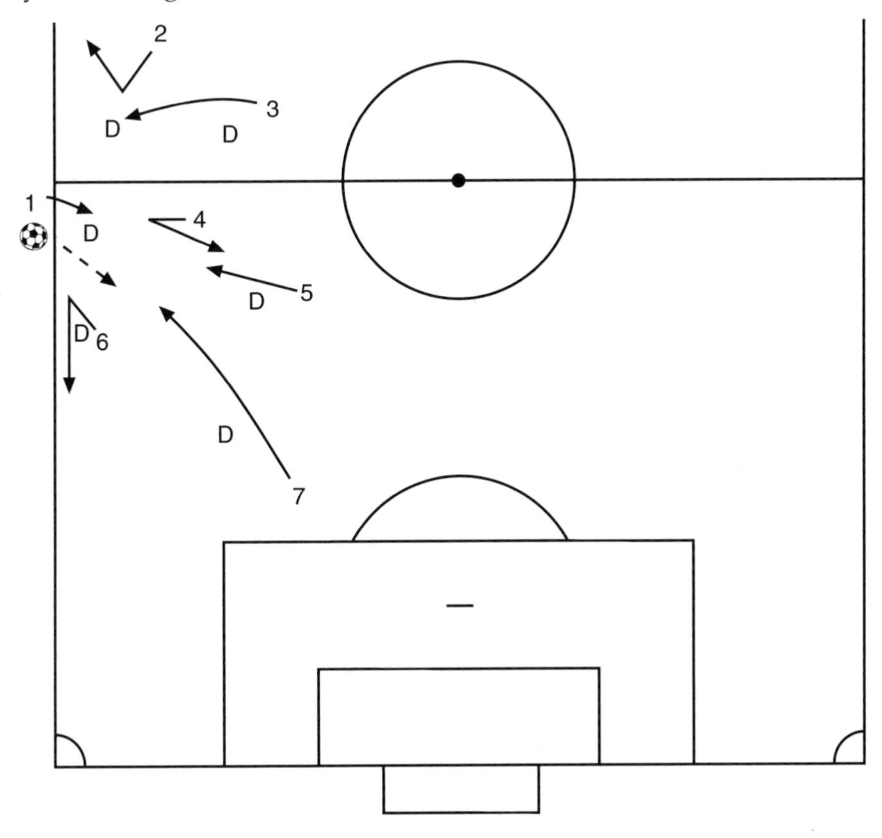

Procedure

2 and 3, 4 and 5, and 6 and 7 work as partners. 2, 4, and 6 check toward 1 and then move away at varying times. When these players move away, 3, 5, and 7 move into the space vacated by each partner. 1 throws in to any of the attackers and immediately moves onto the field to support further play.

Defensive Tips

All defenders must be alert so they are not beaten by the attackers as they move toward and away from the attacker taking the throw-in.

Offensive Tips

Aggressive runs by the attackers are important in order to create defensive confusion and open space for an attacker. The throw-in should be made to the outside of the attacker.

Contributor: Shawn Ladda, Professor of Physical Education, Manhattan College, Riverdale, New York

Flick On to Goal

Formation

Attacker 1 is in position to take the throw-in 25 yards from the goal line. Attacker 3 stands on the midpoint of the six-yard line. Attacker 2 is five yards closer to the near sideline than is 3. Attacker 4 stands on the midpoint of the penalty-area restraining arc. Attacker 5 is 10 yards to the left of 4.

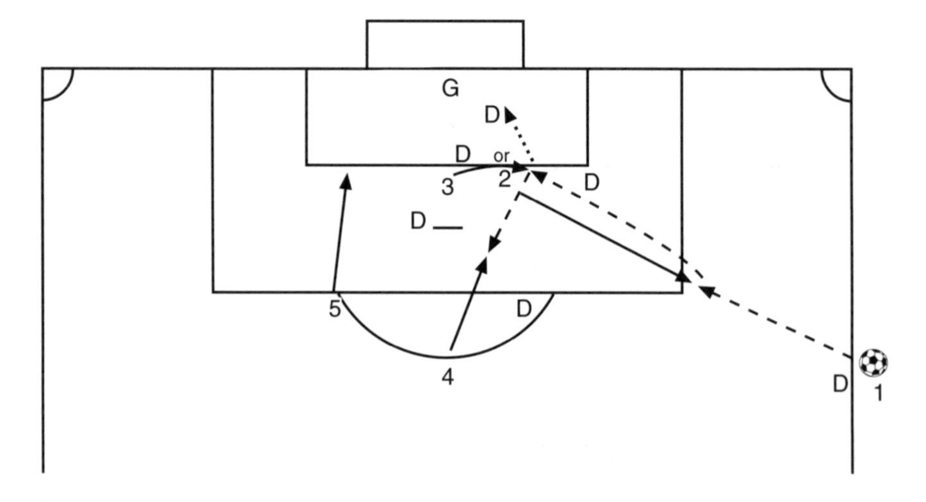

Procedure

2 initiates the throw-in by running toward 1. 1 throws to the head of 2. 2 flicks toward goal to 3, who has moved to the space vacated by 2. 3 turns and either shoots on goal or passes to 4, who has run toward the goal area to be in position for the pass or to handle a possible rebound if 3 shoots on goal. 5 moves toward the goal area to be in position for a possible rebound.

Variation

2 initiates the throw-in by running toward 1. As 3 moves to the space vacated by 2, 1 throws to the head of 2. 2 heads the ball toward the corner to 1, who enters the field immediately after the throw-in. 1, who has moved toward the goal line, crosses the ball to 5, who takes a first-time shot on goal. 4 moves toward the goal area to be in position for a possible rebound.

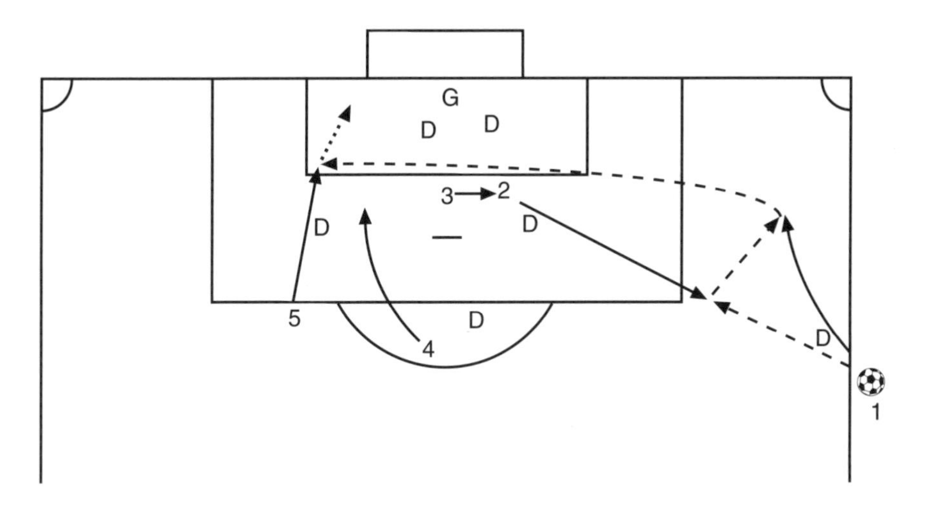

Defensive Tips

This is a dangerous situation for the defense because the attackers cannot be offside on the throw-in. 2's defender covers closely to prevent a numerical advantage for the attack. Defenders must not let attackers get open in the central scoring area. Those defending against 4 and 5 must not let them get goal-side.

Offensive Tips

2's run is important to set up a two-on-one situation with 1 or to create open space for 3.

Contributors: Anson Dorrance, Head Women's Coach, and Bill Palladino, Assistant Women's Coach, University of North Carolina, Chapel Hill, North Carolina

Goalkeeper

Formation In the defensive third of the field, attacker 1 is in position to take the throw-in. Attacker 2 is near the sideline of the penalty area. Attacker 3 is 10 yards up the field from 1. Attacker 4 is square with 1, 15 yards within the field. Attacker 5 is in the center of the penalty area. Attacker 6 is near the opposite sideline. The goalkeeper is by the near post of the goal.

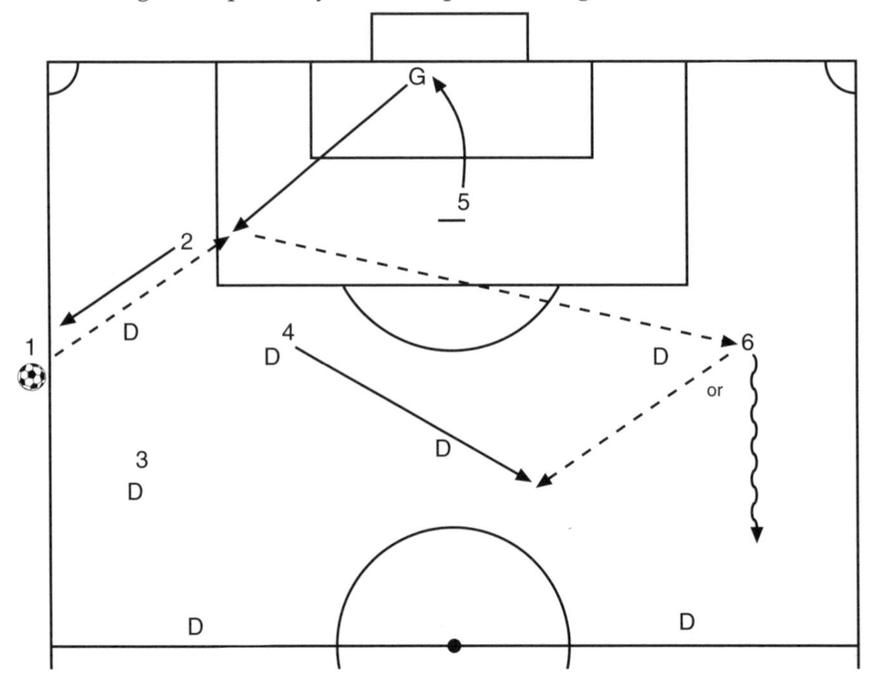

Procedure 2 initiates the throw-in by running toward 1. To catch the throw-in from 1, the goalkeeper runs to the sideline of the penalty area near the space vacated by 2. 5 moves into the near-post goal area. The goalkeeper switches fields by throwing the ball to 6, who carries the ball up the field or passes to 4 who has cut to the middle of the field.

Defensive Tips This is a dangerous situation for the attack. In this area of the field, the defenders can afford to risk losing the attackers they are covering to try to intercept the throw-in and go immediately on attack. If the defenders gain possession of the ball, they must execute quick passes and shots so the opponents don't have time to recover.

Offensive Tips The run by 2 must be quick so that open space is created for the goalkeeper and there is no danger of interception. The goalkeeper must catch the ball above head-height and pass it immediately to 6. If 6 is not open, the goalkeeper can look to 4, and if 4 is not open, can punt the ball well up the field.

Contributors: Mel Schmid, Professor Emeritus, The College of New Jersey, Trenton, New Jersey, and John McKeon, Former Men's Coach, East Stroudsburg State University, East Stroudsburg, Pennsylvania

Great Flick

Formation

Attacker 1 is in position to take the throw-in at the six-yard line extended. Attacker 2 is within the goal area. Attacker 3 is on the penalty spot. Attacker 4 is outside the penalty area on the far side of the field.

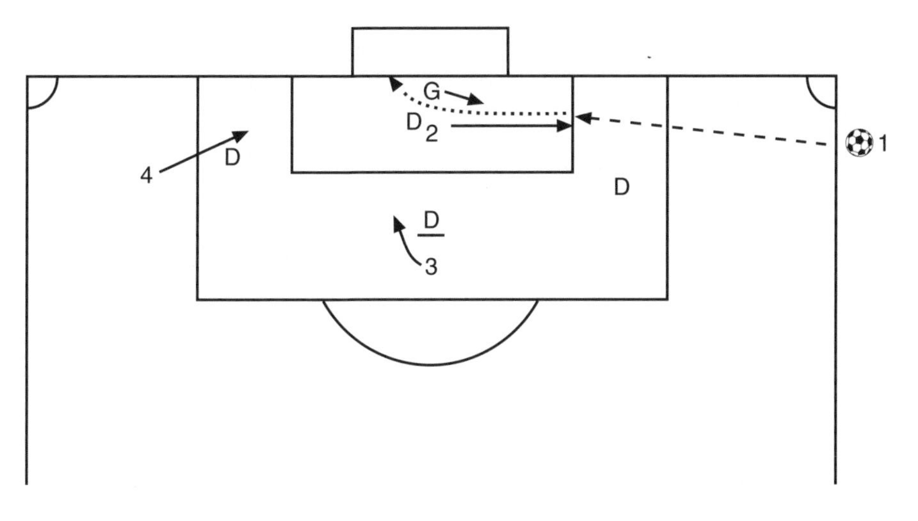

Procedure

2 initiates the play by running to the edge of the goal area. 1 throws the ball to the head of 2 who deflects the ball with the side of the head to the far corner of the goal. 3 and 4 follow up the play to be in position for a rebound.

Defensive Tips

This is a dangerous situation for the defense, particularly if the player taking the throw-in can make a long throw into the goal area. A defender must move with 2 and another defender must come back to cover the defensive area vacated by 2. The defenders must play the ball as high as possible and make a first-time clear out of the area. The goalkeeper must punch the ball out of the area or completely over the goal if it cannot be caught.

Offensive Tips

2's head shot to the far post is made if the goalkeeper leaves this space open by moving toward the near post. If the goalkeeper does not come out, a shot to the near post might be a better choice.

Contributor: John Reeves, Director of Physical Education and Intercollegiate Athletics, Columbia University, New York, New York

Long Thrower

Formation

In the attacking third of the field, attacker 2 is in position to take the throw-in. Attacker 1, who is known to have the ability to take long throw-ins, is on the field, 15 yards away from 2.

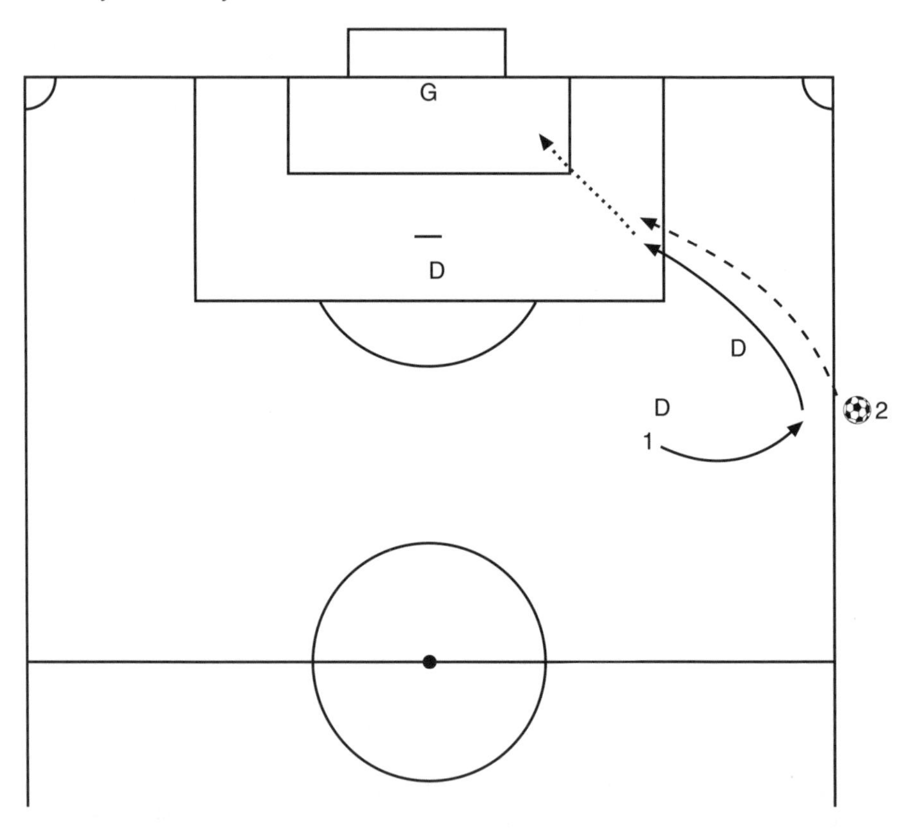

Procedure

1 sprints toward 2, calling that he or she will take the throw-in. 1 nears 2, but then sprints toward the goal. 2 picks up the ball and makes a throw-in to 1 who is on a dead run for the goal. 1 takes a first-time shot on goal.

Defensive Tips

The defenders covering 1 and 2 must communicate with each other and switch coverage if necessary.

Offensive Tips

The success of this play depends on the attack establishing that 1 will take the throw-in, and on 1 and 2 disguising their intentions until the last second.

Contributor: John Reeves, Director of Physical Education and Intercollegiate Athletics, Columbia University, New York, New York

Power

Formation

Attacker 1 is in position to take a throw-in 30 yards from the goal line. Attackers 2 and 3, two tall players, are just outside the six-yard line, five yards apart. Attackers 4, 5, and 6 are in a line on the far side of the penalty area. Attacker 7 is several yards outside the midpoint of the penalty-area restraining arc. Attackers 8 and 9 are at wide positions opposite each other in the attacking side of the field, near the midfield line.

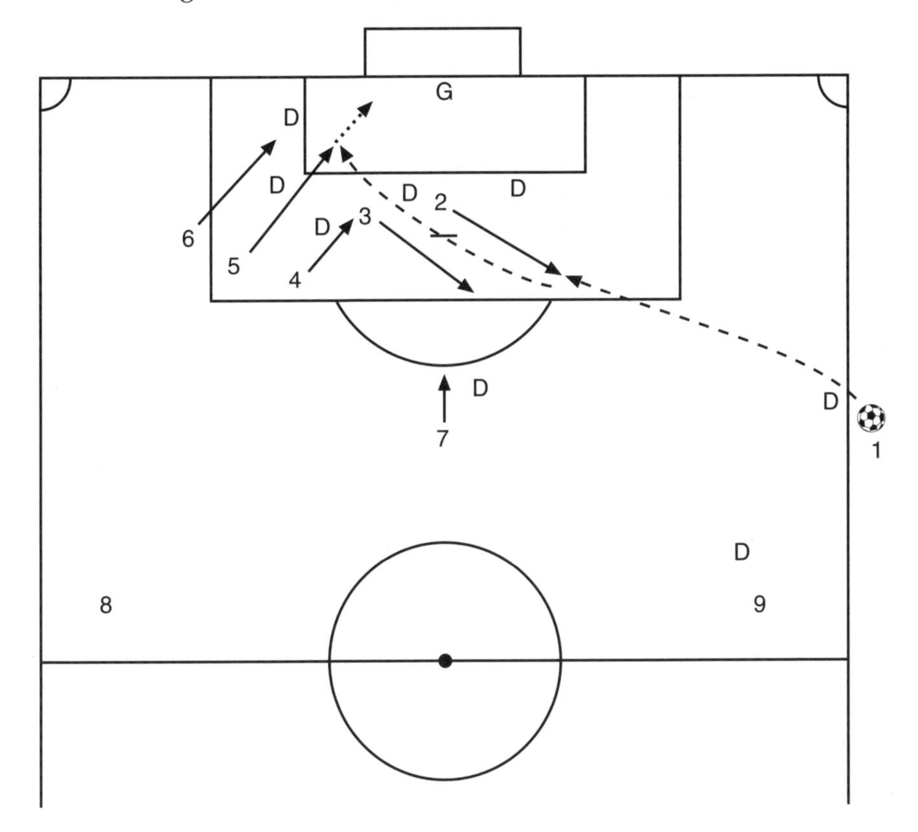

Procedure

1 makes a long throw-in to 2 or 3, who have moved toward the ball but kept their spacing. Whichever player gets it flicks the ball to 4, 5, or 6, who must anticipate the pass and run to the ball. The first player to the ball takes a first-time shot on goal. 7 moves toward the top of the penalty-area restraining arc to be in position for a possible rebound or clear.

continued

Power *(continued)*

Variation

2 and 3 move toward 1 but keep their spacing. If the defense sags in to cover the long throw-in, 1 throws in to 9, who crosses the ball to the far post to 4, 5, or 6, who shoots on goal.

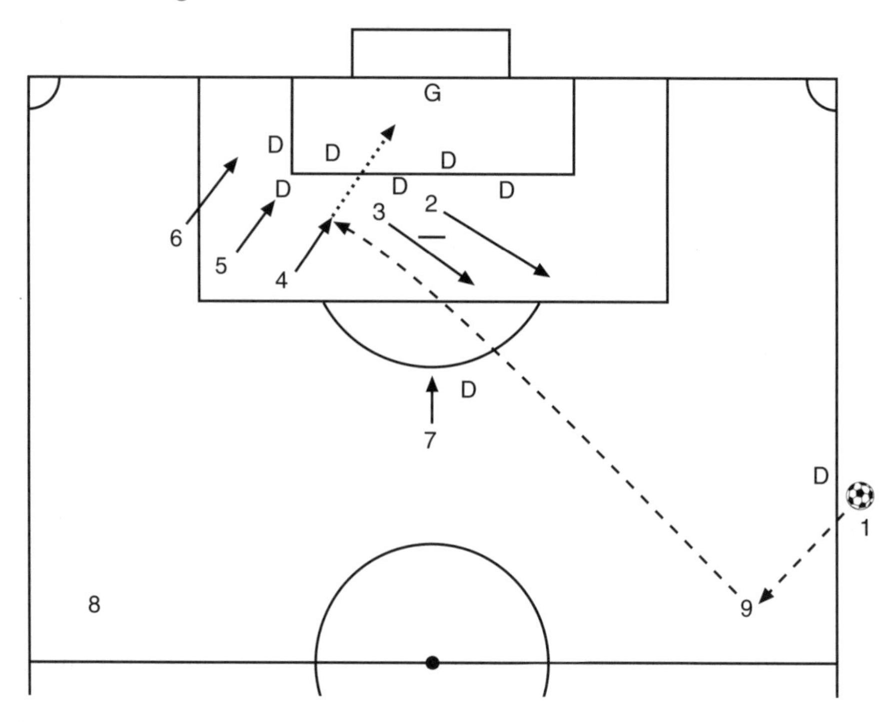

Defensive Tips

This is a dangerous situation for the defense because the attackers cannot be offside on the throw-in. If the player taking the throw-in makes a long throw into the space in front of the goal, the defenders covering 4, 5, and 6, along with the goalkeeper, must not let them get goal-side or open in scoring territory. The defenders must play the ball above head-height and the goalkeeper must punch the ball out of the area if it cannot be caught. The defenders covering 2 and 3 move with them on their runs.

Offensive Tips

The runs made by 2 and 3 are essential to create open space behind them. 4, 5, and 6 must make aggressive runs to be first to the ball. 8 and 9 stay alert for an interception and counterattack. Their job is to slow the attack down until their teammates get back.

Contributor: Brian E. Chafin, Men's Coach, Centre College, Danville, Kentucky

Scissors

Formation

Attacker 1 is in position to take the throw-in at midfield. Attacker 2 lines up square to and 15 yards from 1. Attacker 3 is 15 yards down the line from 1.

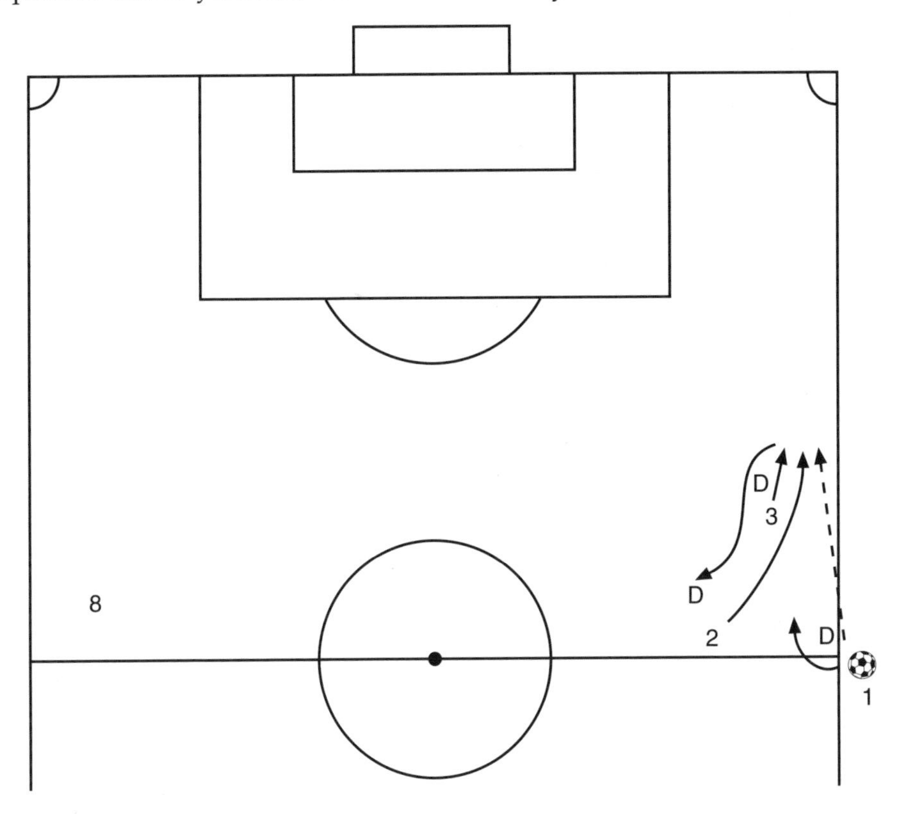

Procedure

3 initiates the throw-in by moving down the line away from 1. 3 then turns and sprints toward the defender marking 2. At the same time, 2 makes a run toward the space vacated by 3. 1, after faking first to 2's initial position inside, throws the ball down the line to 2 and immediately enters the field to support further play.

Defensive Tips

The defenders covering 2 and 3 must communicate and may need to switch coverage to prevent the attackers from getting goal-side.

Offensive Tips

Since the play is designed to lose 2's defender in the "traffic" created by the runs made by 2 and 3, it is important that 3 runs toward 2's defender and not 2.

Contributor: Nick D. Sansom, Men's Coach, State University of New York at Stony Brook, Stony Brook, New York

Screen and Go

Formation

In the defensive third of the field, attacker 1 is in position to take the throw-in. Attacker 2 is near the sideline 10 yards upfield from 1. Attacker 3 is 15 yards within the field, square with 1. Attacker 4 is midway between the near corners of the penalty and goal areas. The goalkeeper is by the near-post area of the goal.

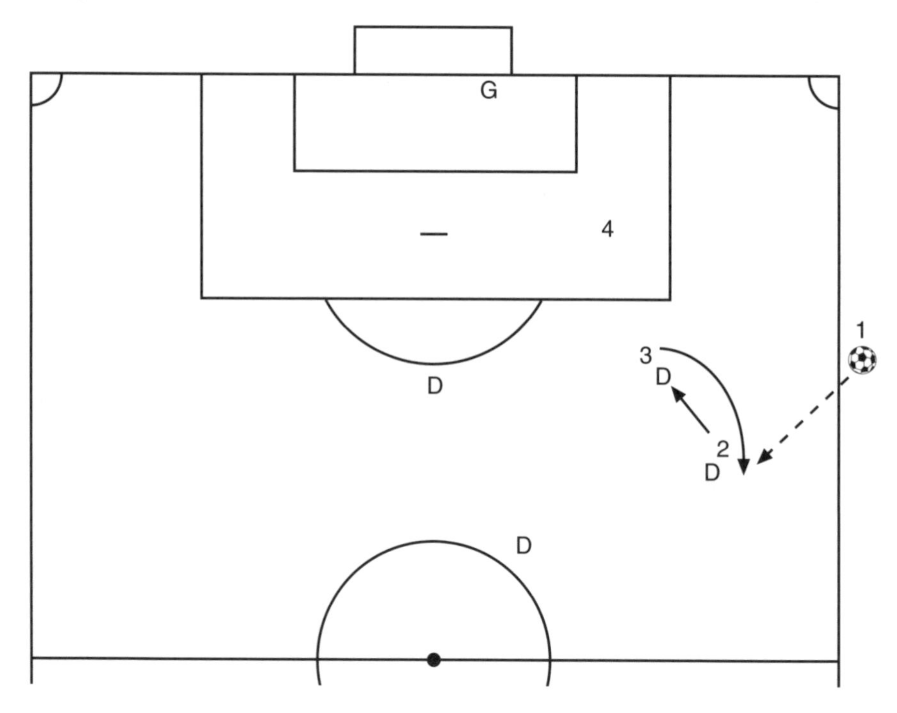

Procedure

2 initiates the play by running to screen (not obstruct) 3's defender. 3 breaks away from the defender and sprints to receive the throw-in from 1.

Defensive Tips

This is a dangerous area for the attack. The defenders can take chances to intercept the throw-in and move immediately on attack.

Offensive Tips

If 2's defender moves to stay with 2, 3 sprints upfield behind the defender. If the defenders covering 2 and 3 switch, 3 cuts down the sideline in front of the defender.

Contributors: Mel Schmid, Professor Emeritus, The College of New Jersey, and John McKeon, Former Men's Coach, East Stroudsburg State University, East Stroudsburg, Pennsylvania

Soccer Line Go

Formation

Attacker 1 is in position to take the throw-in near midfield. Attackers 2, 3, 4, and 5 are in a line from left to right, 15 yards outside the right side of the 18-yard line. Attacker 6 is at midfield, 10 yards from 1.

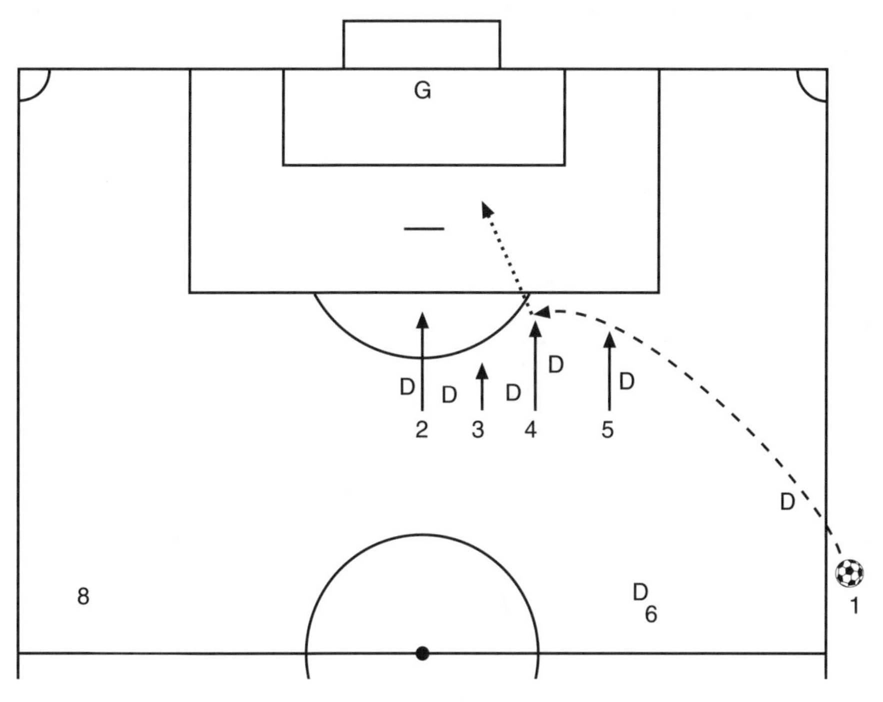

Procedure

On a predetermined signal, 2, 3, 4, and 5 sprint to the open space past their defenders. 1 makes the throw-in to this open space for any attacker to control and shoot on goal.

Defensive Tips

Since the attackers cannot be offside on the throw-in, this is a dangerous situation for the defense—particularly if the player taking the throw-in can make a long throw in front of the goal. The defenders covering 2, 3, 4, and 5 must not let them get goal-side. The goalkeeper must clear the ball out of the area if it cannot be caught.

Offensive Tips

A quick attack is essential so the defense does not have time to recover. 2, 3, 4, and 5 must make aggressive runs to get goal-side of their defenders and be first to the ball.

Contributor: John A. Reeves, Director of Physical Education and Intercollegiate Athletics, Columbia University, New York, New York

Throw to Score

Formation

Attacker 1 is in position to take the throw-in 20 yards from the goal line. Attackers 2 and 3 are at the far and near posts, respectively. Attackers 4, 5, 6, and 7 are in an echelon formation at the far corner of the penalty area. Attackers 8 and 9 are near midfield, about 10 yards apart.

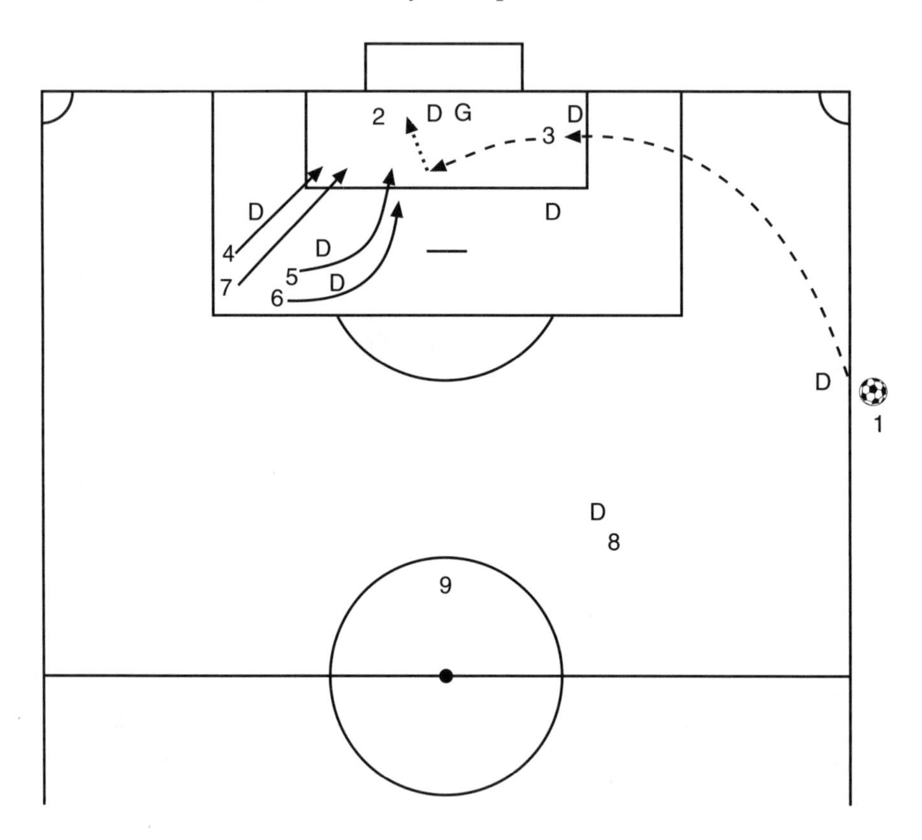

Procedure

1 throws toward the far or near post for 2 or 3. Whoever gets the ball either shoots directly on goal or deflects the ball back toward 4, 5, 6, and 7, who are charging toward the goal area. If the ball is deflected back, whoever gets the ball takes a shot on goal. The others stay alert for a possible rebound.

Variation

1 throws to the space between the echelon and the goalkeeper as the players in the echelon are moving toward the goal. The first player to get the ball takes a first-time shot on goal.

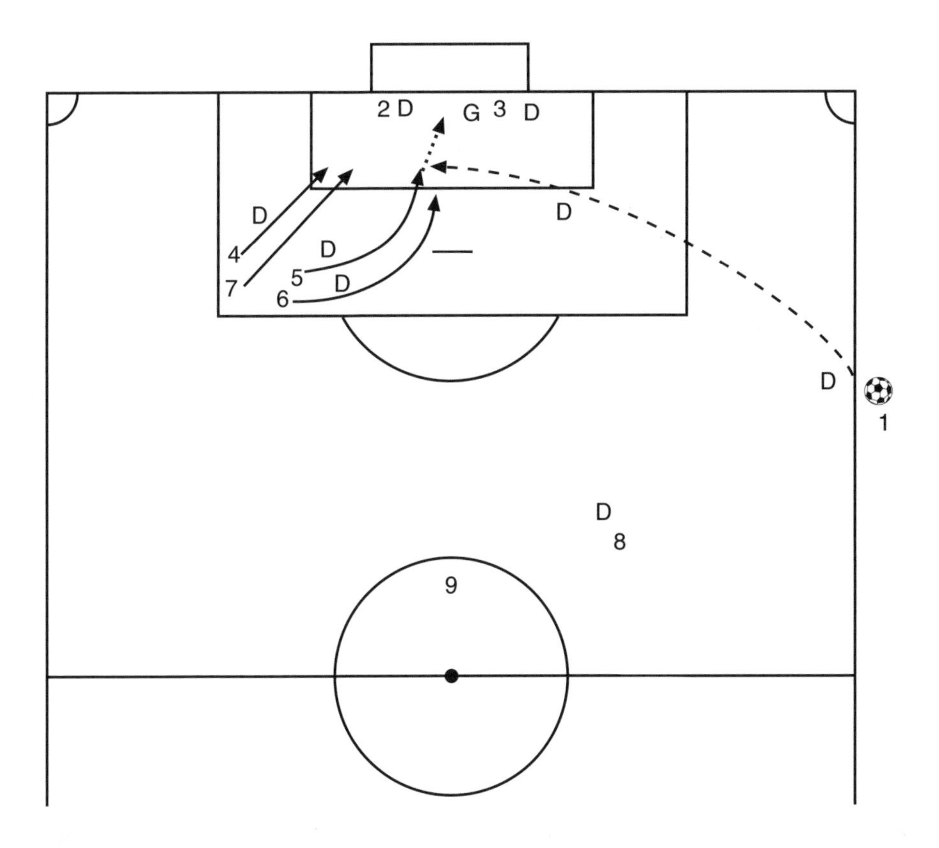

Defensive Tips

Since the attackers cannot be offside on the throw-in, this is a dangerous situation for the defenders, particularly if the player taking the throw-in can throw the ball into scoring territory. The goalkeeper must play the ball as high as possible and clear it out of the area if it cannot be caught. Those defending against 4, 5, 6, and 7 must not let them get goal-side.

Offensive Tips

4, 5, 6, and 7 must make aggressive runs to be first to the ball.

Contributor: John A. Reeves, Director of Physical Education and Intercollegiate Athletics, Columbia University, New York, New York

Top Flick

Formation

Attacker 1 is in position to take the throw-in 10 yards from the corner of the field. Attackers 2 and 4 stand at the near and far posts, respectively. Attackers 3, 5, and 6 are spread out in a line just outside the six-yard line.

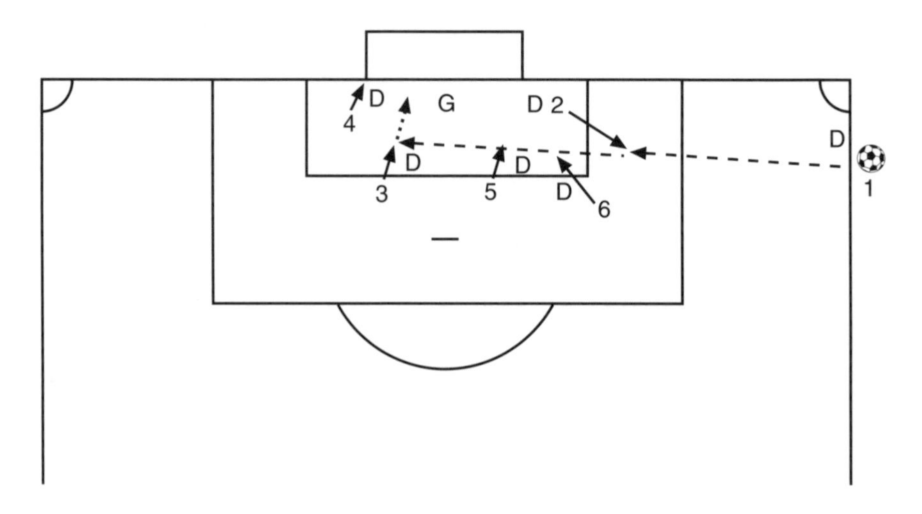

Procedure

2 sprints toward a predetermined spot outside the near corner of the goal area. 1 throws the ball to 2's head. 2 flicks the ball toward 3, 4, 5, or 6, who are sprinting toward predetermined positions. The first player to get the ball takes a first-time shot on goal.

Defensive Tips

This is a dangerous situation since the attackers cannot be offside on the throw-in, which should be treated like a corner kick. A defender stays with 2 to prevent a numerical advantage for the attack. The defenders covering 3, 4, 5, and 6 must not let them be unmarked in the central scoring area. The goalkeeper must punch the ball out of the area if it cannot be caught.

Offensive Tips

If 2's defender does not move out with him or her, 1 can throw-in to 2 and set up a two-on-one situation. 3, 4, 5, and 6 must be first to the ball.

Contributor: Tom G. McLoughlin, Men's Coach, Fairleigh Dickinson University, Florham-Madison Campus, Madison, New Jersey

Kickoff Tactics

The kickoff occurs in dead-ball situations to start play at the beginning of the game, to restart play at the beginning of the second half and any overtime periods, and after either team scores a goal.

Rules for Kickoffs

A kickoff starts play at the beginning of a game and restarts play in the second half, for any overtime periods, and after a goal is scored. The kickoff that follows a goal is taken by the team scored upon. The play is made by kicking a stationary ball set at the center of the field into the opponent's half of the field. All players must be in their half of the field, and every player opposing the kicker must be at least 10 yards from the ball until it is kicked off. A ball is kicked off when it travels forward. A goal may be scored directly from a kickoff. As with all restarts, the kicker may not play the ball again until it has been touched or played by another player.

Defensive Tactics

On the kickoff, the offensive team should not allow the defenders the opportunity to get a psychological advantage by gaining possession. This is particularly true when the kickoff follows a goal. To maximize the possibility of gaining or regaining the ball, defenders should try to anticipate where the attackers will pass it and react quickly to cut off passing lanes. As soon as the attacking team touches the ball, one or more defenders rush to pressure the player controlling it, and the other defenders stay alert for passes.

Attacking Tactics

There are two basic—but different—attack objectives for the kickoff. One is to accomplish quick and deep penetration into the final third of the field, putting immediate pressure on the defense and creating a scoring opportunity. The other is to retain possession of the ball, giving the team's players confidence early in the game.

The attacking team seeks to find gaps in the defense and take advantage of any lack of concentration by defenders. On quick opening plays, attackers must move quickly toward the goal to catch the defenders in the attacking third of the field by surprise. Success depends on attackers' making aggressive runs to open space and getting goal-side of the defenders. These attackers must be able to receive air passes on the run and make volley or quick control passes or shots on goal. On developing plays, the attackers move the ball in an attempt to create and exploit a numerical advantage. The success of these plays depends on good ball control, accurate passes, and not holding the ball too long. On all plays, the attackers must be purposeful and keep alert to prevent an attack on their own goal should the defense gain possession of the ball.

Kickoff Plays

The success of quick opening plays depends on attackers not involved in the initial action getting goal-side of the defenders. The success of developing plays depends on good ball control and crisp, accurate passing. The attackers involved in the initial play must be close to each other so their passes will be quick enough to prevent the defense from intercepting the ball.

Some teams may choose not to use a set kickoff play, opting instead to develop spontaneous play from the field. The 10 kickoff plays in this chapter are presented for those of you who wish to have a set plan for this situation. Each of the plays can be started to the opposite side.

Back and Forth

Formation

Attackers 1, 2, and 3 are in position to take the kickoff. Attackers 4 and 5 are on the right and left sides, respectively, of the midfield line. Attackers 6, 7, and 8 are at midfield positions.

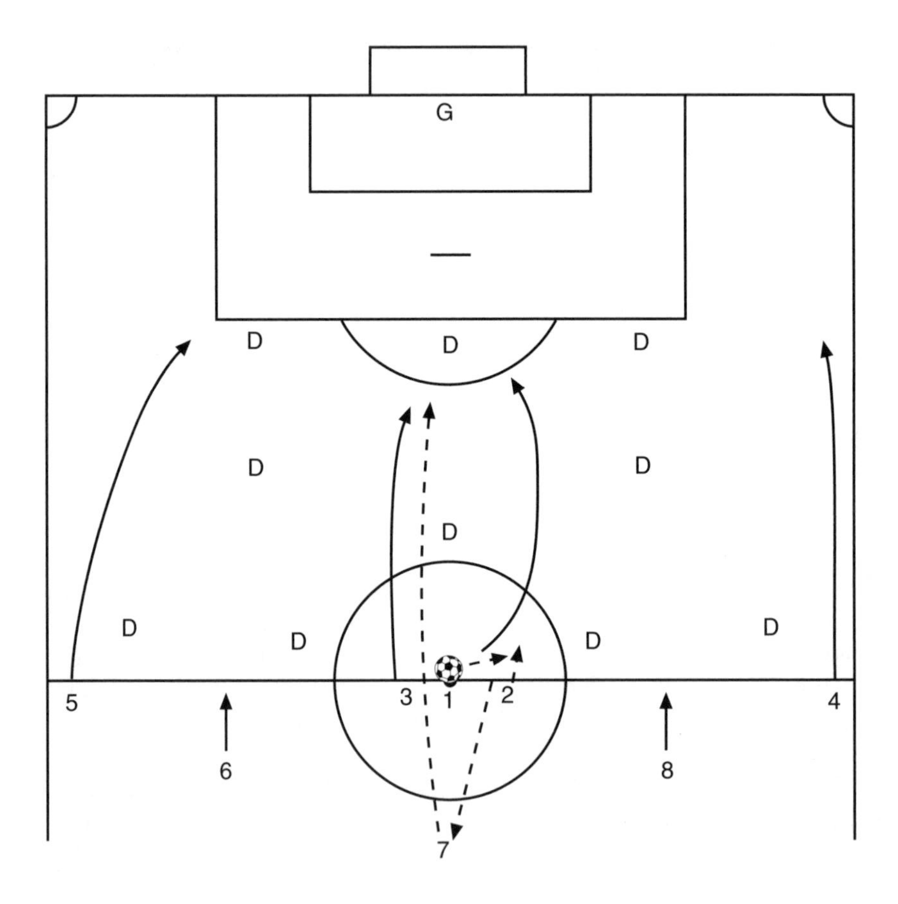

Procedure

1 passes to 2, who immediately passes back to 7. 7 makes a long pass upfield to 1, 3, 4, or 5, who is moving toward the goal. 4 and 5 are cutting in toward the goal on their runs. 6 and 8 follow the play.

Variation

1 passes to 2, who immediately passes back to 7. 7 makes a long pass upfield to either 4 or 5 on the wings, who centers the ball to the goal area for the other attackers.

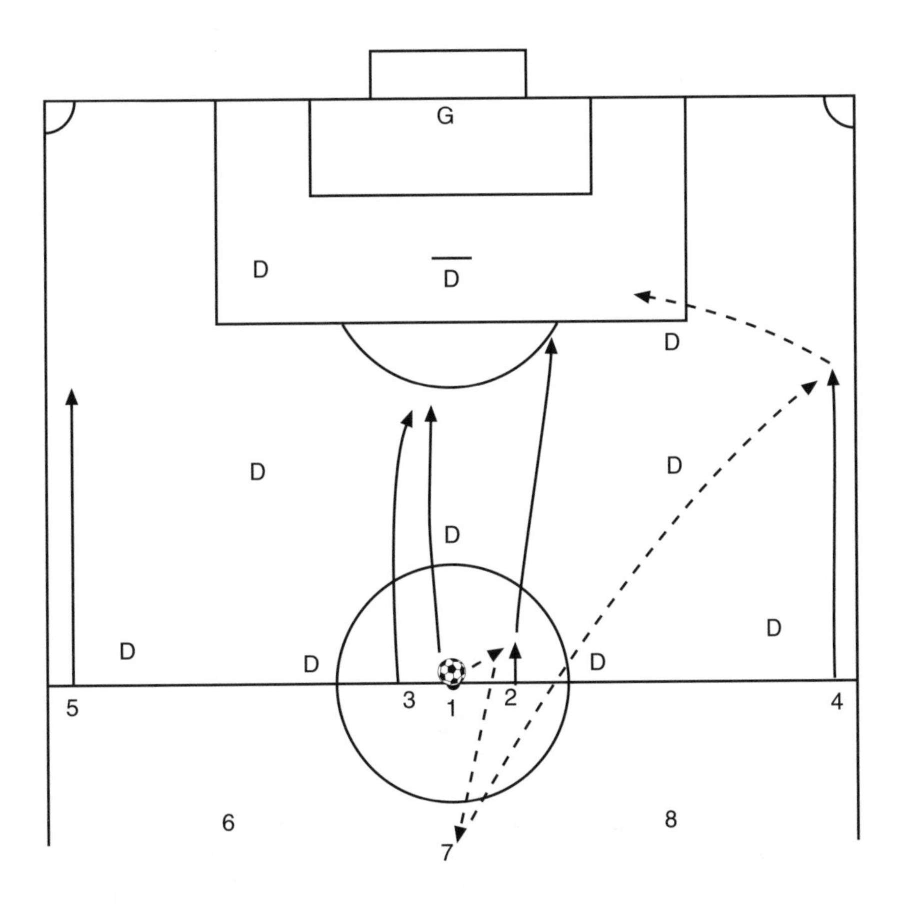

Defensive Tips

The three defenders around the kickoff circle predetermine where each will move on the kickoff. One defender pressures the player with the ball; the others attempt to intercept passes. All defenders try to anticipate where the ball might be passed.

Offensive Tips

7 may choose to dribble and draw an opponent before passing.

Contributor: Irv Schmid, Former Men's Coach, Springfield College, Springfield, Massachusetts

Center

Formation Attackers 1, 2, and 3 are in position to take the kickoff. Attackers 4 and 5 are on the right and left sides, respectively, of the midfield line. Attackers 6, 7, and 8 are at midfield positions.

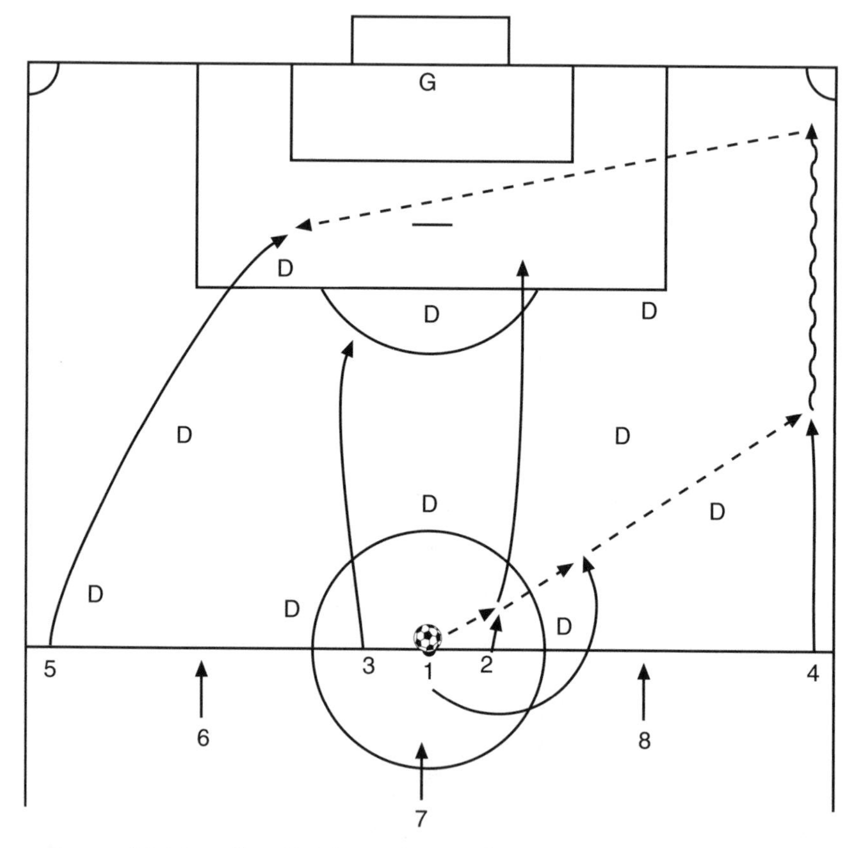

Procedure 1 kicks off to 2. 2 hesitates and then passes the ball between the defenders back to 1, who has cut behind 2 to get into position for the pass. 1 passes to 4, who has sprinted down the wing. 4 dribbles toward the baseline and centers the ball to 2, 3, and 5, who are sprinting toward the goal. 6, 7, and 8 follow the play.

Defensive Tips The three defenders around the kickoff circle predetermine where each will move on the kickoff. One defender pressures the player with the ball; the others attempt to intercept passes. All defenders try to anticipate where the ball might be passed.

Offensive Tips The success of this play depends on good ball control, accurate passing, and not holding the ball too long. 6, 7, and 8 stay ready to go on defense if the opponents gain possession and counterattack.

Contributor: Irv Schmid, Former Men's Coach, Springfield College, Springfield, Massachusetts

Cross

Formation Attackers 1, 2, and 3 are in position to take the kickoff. Attackers 4 and 5 are on the right and left sides, respectively, of the midfield line. Attackers 6, 7, and 8 are at midfield positions.

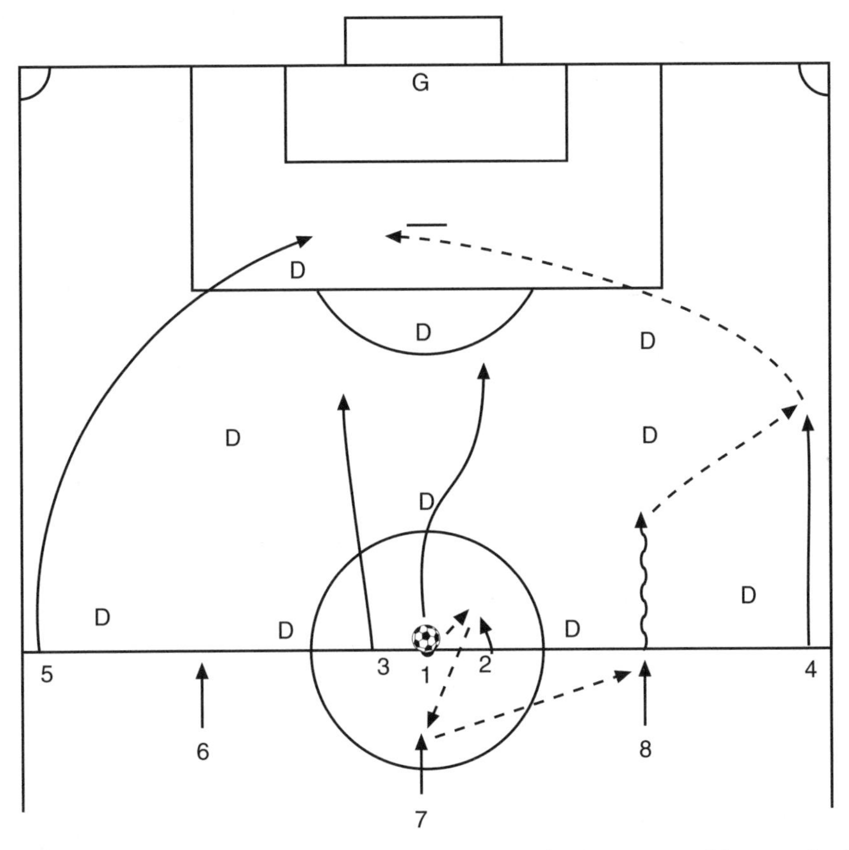

Procedure 1 kicks off to 2. 2 passes back to 7, who has moved forward a few steps to receive the ball. 7 passes to 8, who dribbles to draw a defender before passing to 4. 4 crosses the ball to 5, who is sprinting toward the goal area. 6 and 7 follow the play.

Defensive Tips The three defenders around the kickoff circle predetermine where each will move on the kickoff. One defender pressures the player with the ball; the others attempt to intercept passes. All defenders try to anticipate where the ball might be passed.

Offensive Tips The success of this play depends on good ball control, accurate passing, and not holding the ball too long. 6, 7, and 8 stay alert, ready to go on defense if the opponent gains possession and counterattacks.

Contributor: Irv Schmid, Former Men's Coach, Springfield College, Springfield, Massachusetts

Defenders' Boost

Formation

This restart play, unlike all the others in this book, is designed for the defense. Attackers 1, 2, and 3 are in position to take the kickoff. Attackers 4 and 5 are at the right and left sides, respectively, of the midfield line. Attackers 6, 7, and 8 are at midfield positions. Defenders 1, 2, 3, and 4 are around the perimeter of the center circle. Defenders 5 and 6 are positioned 5 yards inside and 5 yards behind the left and right sides, respectively, of the midfield line.

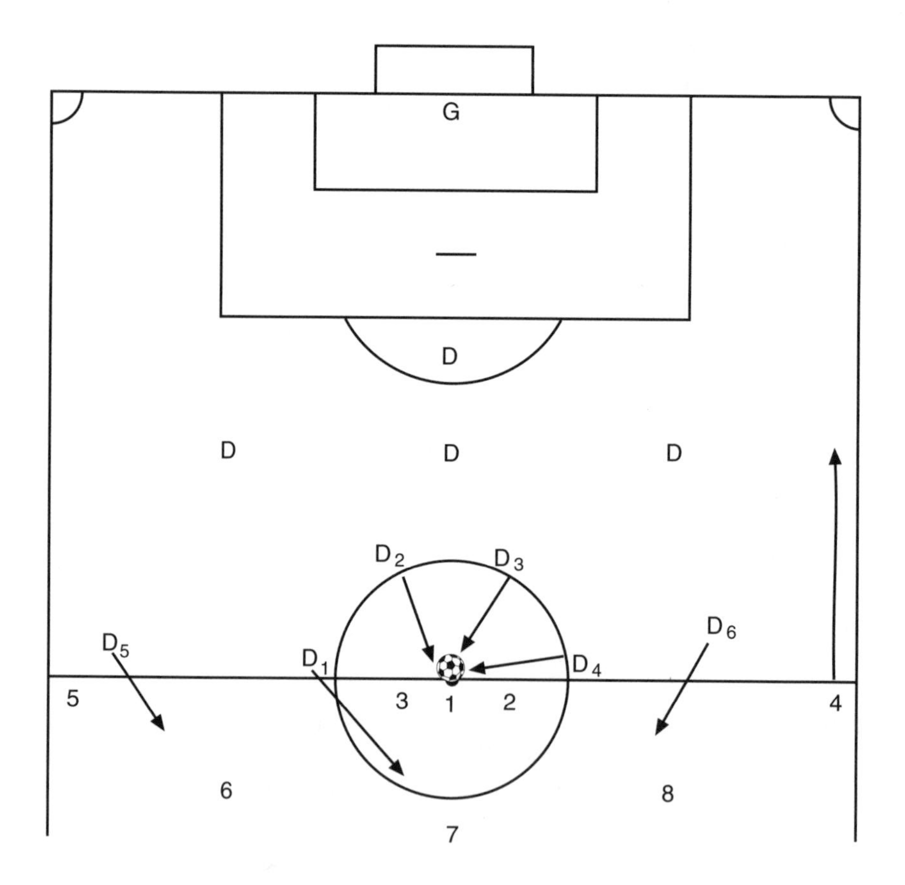

Procedure

The moment the ball is moved forward by an attacker, defenders 2, 3, and 4 charge the ball, attempting to gain possession. Defender 1 moves toward the attacking midfielders to prevent a back pass. Defenders 5 and 6 move to cut off passing lanes to the wings.

Defensive Tips

Some teams are careless on kickoffs, especially following a goal, when the team scored upon tends to be psychologically down. This may be a good time for the defenders to put immediate pressure on the attackers. Should the defense gain possession of the ball on the kickoff, they must take advantage of the situation and counterattack immediately. They must also be alert and ready to defend if they do not intercept the ball.

Offensive Tips

Attackers must never be haphazard about the kickoff. Even if they do not use a specific kickoff play, they must be careful to make accurate passes and not hold onto the ball too long. Attacking midfielders and backs must be alert and ready to slow down a counterattack should the defense intercept the ball.

Contributor: John Reeves, Director of Physical Education and Intercollegiate Athletics, Columbia University, New York, New York

Forward Options

Formation Attackers 1, 2, and 3 are in position to take the kickoff. Attackers 4 and 5 are on the right and left sidelines of midfield, respectively. Attackers 6, 7, and 8 are at midfield positions.

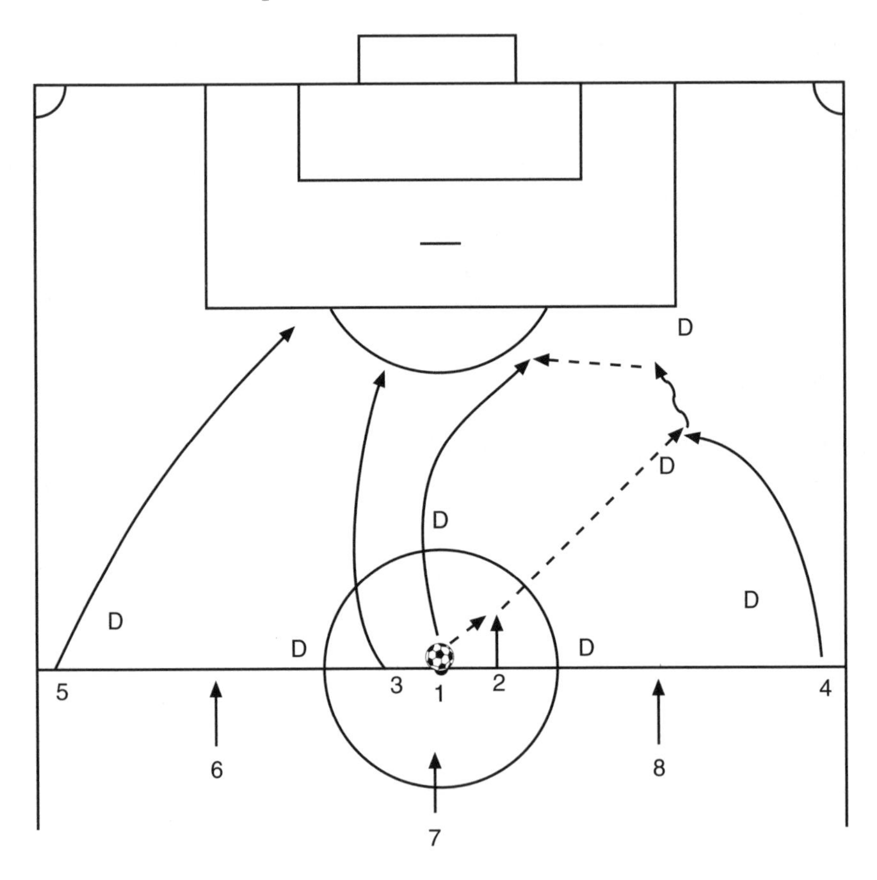

Procedure 1 passes to 2, who moves forward to receive the pass. 2 makes a long pass to 4, who is cutting inward while running down the field. 4 receives the ball, dribbles toward the goal until drawing an opponent, and passes to 1 or 5, who are moving toward goal. 6, 7, and 8 follow the play.

Defensive Tips The three defenders around the kickoff circle predetermine where each will move on the kickoff. One defender pressures the player with the ball; the others attempt to intercept passes. All defenders try to anticipate where the ball might be passed.

Offensive Tips 2 may pass to 5 if this attacker has gotten goal-side of the defenders or if 4 is unable to get open.

Contributor: John Reeves, Director of Physical Education and Intercollegiate Athletics, Columbia University, New York, New York

Halfback

Formation Attackers 1, 2, and 3 are in position to take the kickoff. Attackers 4 and 5 are on the right and left sides, respectively, of the midfield line. Attackers 6, 7, and 8 are at midfield positions.

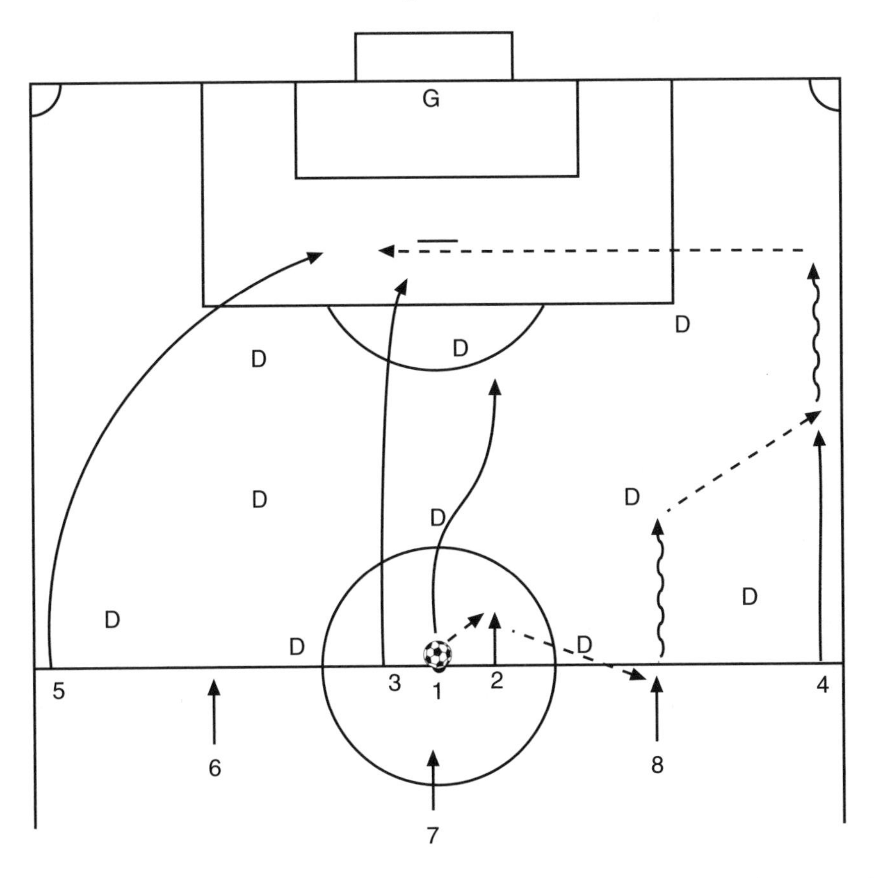

Procedure 1 kicks off to 2, 2 passes to 8, who is moving forward to meet the ball. 8 dribbles forward until drawing a defender, then passes to 4, who has been moving up the wing. 4 centers the ball to 3 and 5, who are sprinting toward goal.

Defensive Tips The three defenders around the kickoff circle predetermine where each will move on the kickoff. One defender pressures the player with the ball; the others attempt to intercept passes. All defenders try to anticipate where the ball might be passed.

Offensive Tips If 4 is tightly covered, 8 may cross the ball to 5.

Contributor: Irv Schmid, Former Men's Coach, Springfield College, Springfield, Massachusetts

Penetrate Deep

Formation Attackers 1 and 2 are in position to take the kickoff. Attackers 4 and 5 are at the right and left sides, respectively, of the midfield line. Attacker 3 is on the midfield line, midway between attackers 1 and 5. Attackers 6, 7, and 8 are at midfield positions.

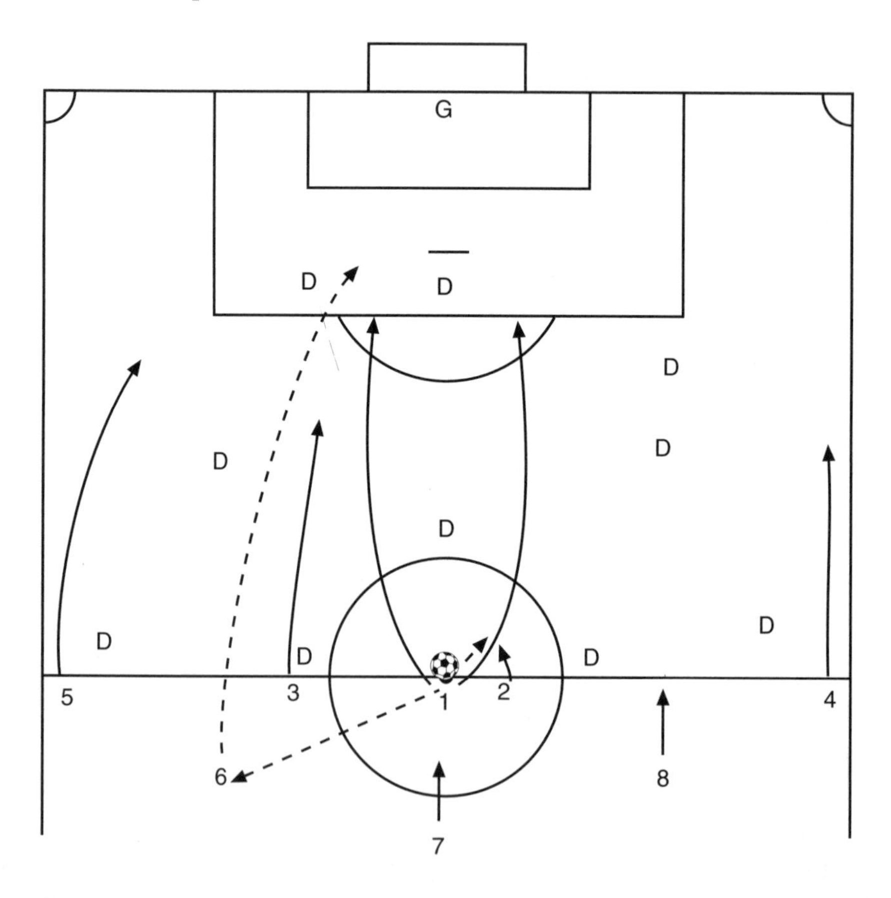

Procedure 1 passes to 2, who immediately passes back to 6. 6 sends a lofted pass to 1, 2, 3, 4, or 5.

Defensive Tips The defenders around the circle move to pressure the player with the ball and cut off passes. Other defenders try to anticipate where a pass might go and move to intercept the ball or slow down the attack.

Offensive Tips 1, 2, 3, 4, and 5 must make aggressive runs to penetrate deeply into scoring territory. The ability to receive the ball in the air and take quick shots on goal is critical for the success of this play.

Contributor: John Reeves, Director of Physical Education and Intercollegiate Athletics, Columbia University, New York, New York

Quick Opener

Formation

Attackers 1, 2, and 3 are in position to take the kickoff. Attackers 4 and 5 are on the right and left sides, respectively, of the midfield line.

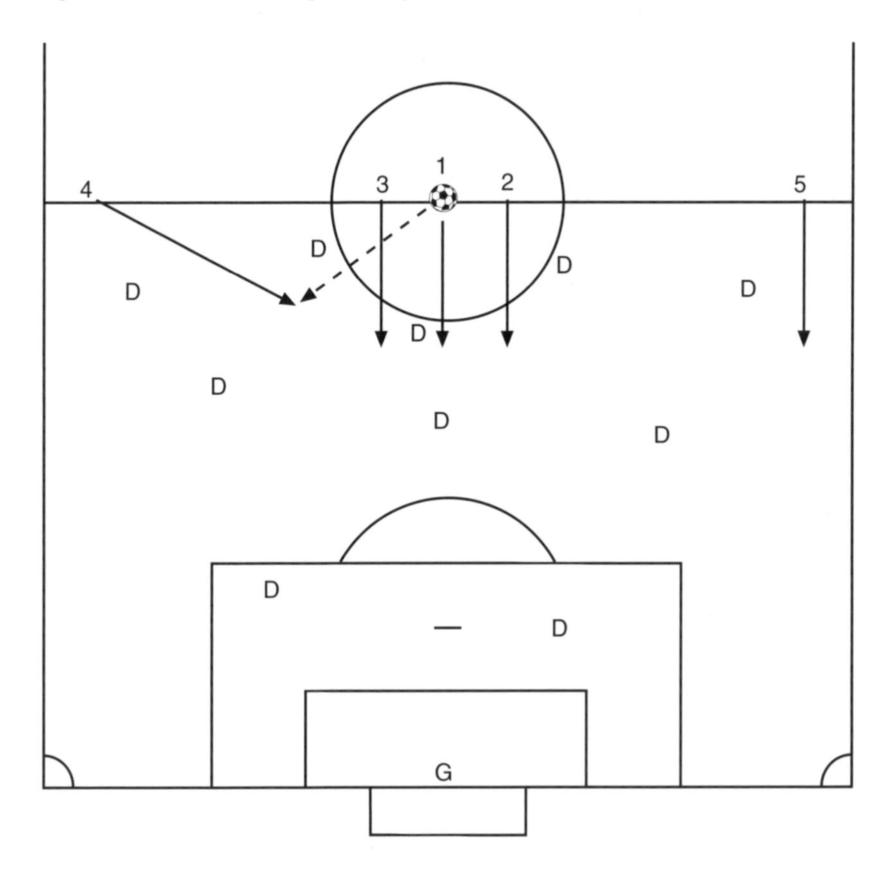

Procedure

1 passes directly to 4, who cuts diagonally between defenders to receive the pass. 4 looks first to pass the ball to any attacker on a breakaway but may instead charge toward the goal or veer out to the sideline and down the wing. The other attackers move forward immediately after the pass.

continued

Variation

1 passes directly to 4, who cuts diagonally forward between defenders. On the pass, 3 cuts behind 4 and moves down the sideline. 1 sprints straight forward. 2 and 5 move diagonally forward and interchange positions. On receiving the pass, 4 looks first to pass to any attacker on a breakaway but may instead charge toward the goal, pass the ball out to either wing, or work a give-and-go with 1.

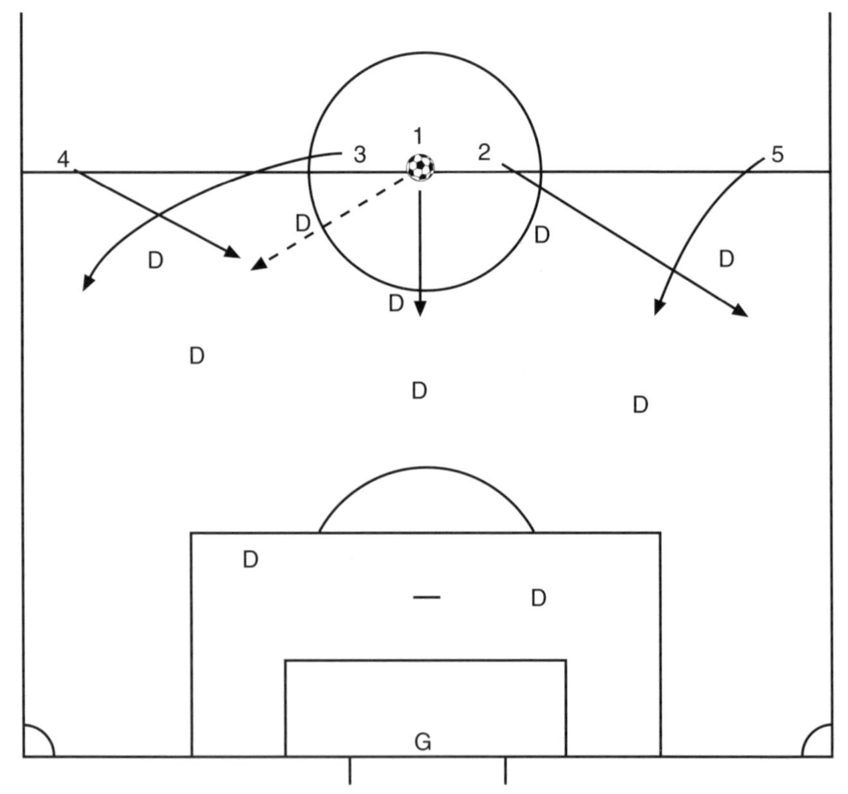

Defensive Tips

The three defenders around the kickoff circle predetermine where each will move on the kickoff. One defender pressures the player with the ball; the others attempt to intercept passes. All defenders try to anticipate where the ball might be passed.

Offensive Tips

The success of this play depends on crisp, accurate passes. 1's pass must be paced to reach the space between defenders at the same time as 4, who must sprint to receive the pass. 1, 2, 3, and 5 sprint forward to receive a pass from 4, put immediate pressure on the defense, and get a quick shot on goal.

Contributor: J. Malcolm Simon, Professor and Director Emeritus of Physical Education and Athletics, New Jersey Institute of Technology, Newark, New Jersey

Switch Field

Formation Attackers 1, 2, and 3 are in position to take the kickoff. Attackers 4 and 5 are on the right and left sides, respectively, of the midfield line.

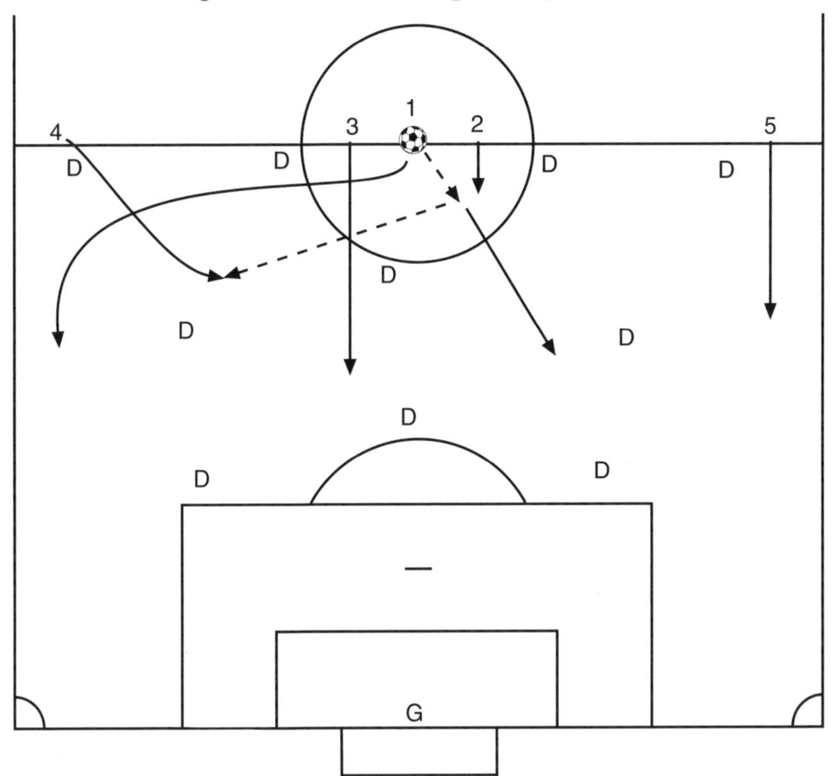

Procedure 1 kicks off to 2, who moves forward to receive the pass. 1 cuts diagonally forward to an advance wing position on the right sideline. 2 passes to 4, who has cut diagonally forward between defenders. After 2's pass, 2, 3, and 5 sprint forward. On receiving the pass, 4 looks first to pass to any attacker on a breakaway but may instead charge toward the goal, pass the ball out to either wing, or work a give-and-go with 3.

Defensive Tips The three defenders around the kickoff circle predetermine where each will move on the kickoff. One defender pressures the player with the ball; the others attempt to intercept passes. All defenders try to anticipate where the ball might be passed.

Offensive Tips The success of this play depends on crisp, accurate passes. 2's pass to 4 must be paced so that the ball and 4 reach the area between defenders at the same time. 1 and 4 maintain the positions they have switched to until an opportune time to switch back.

Contributor: J. Malcolm Simon, Professor and Director Emeritus of Physical Education and Athletics, New Jersey Institute of Technology, Newark, New Jersey

Weave

Formation Attackers 1, 2, and 3 are in position to take the kickoff. Attackers 4 and 5 are on the right and left sides, respectively, of the midfield line.

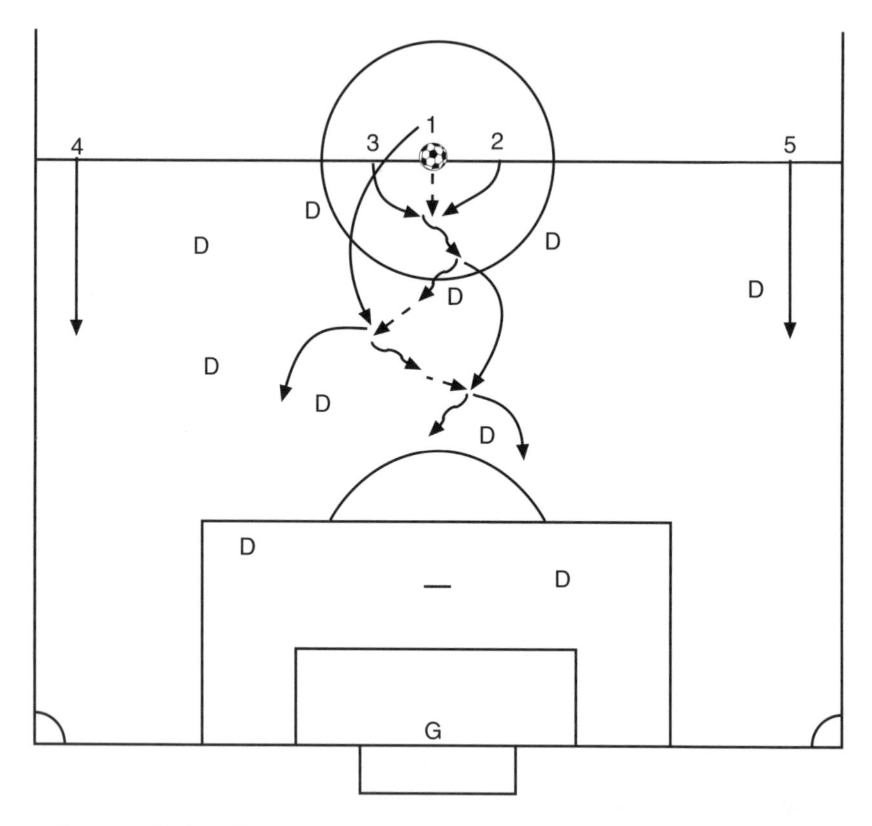

Procedure 1 kicks off to 3, who moves diagonally forward to receive the pass. As 3 dribbles diagonally forward, 1 runs behind 3. 3 passes to 2, who reverses the diagonal dribble movement and passes to 1, who has cut back to receive the pass. Play continues in this "weave" fashion until any of the players can execute a breakthrough. 4 and 5 make straight runs down the wing, keeping wide positions.

Defensive Tips The three defenders around the kickoff circle predetermine where each will move on the kickoff. One defender pressures the player with the ball; the others attempt to intercept passes. All defenders try to anticipate where the ball might be passed.

Offensive Tips The success of this play depends on good ball control, accurate passing, and not holding the ball too long.

Contributor: J. Malcolm Simon, Professor and Director Emeritus of Physical Education and Athletics, New Jersey Institute of Technology, Newark, New Jersey

About the Editors

J. Malcolm Simon

Malcolm Simon and John Reeves combine more than 50 years of soccer coaching expertise in their newest coaching guide. Two of America's top coaches, Simon and Reeves are the editors of five other highly acclaimed Human Kinetics soccer books: *Soccer Restart Plays, Select Soccer Drills, The Coaches' Collection of Soccer Drills, The Soccer Games Book,* and *Practice Games for Winning Soccer.*

Malcolm Simon is professor and director emeritus of physical education and athletics at the New Jersey Institute of Technology (NJIT). He coached soccer, basketball, tennis, and volleyball in college, camp, and YMCA settings for almost 50 years. His soccer teams include National Association of Intercollegiate Athletics (NAIA) national champions and runners-up. Sixteen of his players have been named All-Americans, and five have gone on to play professional soccer nationally and internationally. A graduate of Panzer College (now Montclair State University), Simon received his alma mater's Alumni Honor Award in 1982. Upon his retirement from NJIT in 1994, he was awarded the university's Allan R. Cullimore Medal for Distinguished Service.

John A. Reeves

Twice the Conference Coach of the Year and twice the New Jersey College Coach of the Year, John Reeves achieved a remarkable 172-84-28 record in his 20 years as a collegiate soccer coach, leading his teams to three conference championships. He created and directed two extremely successful summer soccer schools, one at Drew University and one at the University of Rochester, each serving hundreds of youngsters each summer. A past president of the Intercollegiate Soccer Association of America and a member of the National Soccer Coaches Association of America, Reeves is the director of physical education and intercollegiate athletics at Columbia University, where he earned his doctoral degree in 1983. He is a member of the National Collegiate Athletic Association's Division I Men's Soccer Committee.

Simon and Reeves were inducted into the New Jersey Soccer Coaches Association Hall of Fame in 1995.